125 Cool Inventions

SEABREACHER J, PAGE 35

NATIONAL GEOGRAPHIC KiDS

WASHINGTON, D.C.

CARGONAUT, PAGE 31

125 Cool Inventions

NATIONAL
GEOGRAPHIC
KiDS

WASHINGTON, D.C.

CONTENTS

LIGHT CYCLE,
PAGE 32

MARTIN
JETPACK,
PAGE 16

INTRODUCTION

UNO ELECTRIC VEHICLE, PAGE 100

OSTRICH PILLOWS, PAGE 44

FINGERTIP CAMERA, PAGE 49

Welcome to the fascinating, mind-blowing, and incredible world of amazing inventions. Flip through these pages to find 125 of National Geographic Kids' favorite innovative ideas, from cutting-edge concoctions to visionary vehicles! Discover the high-tech camera that fits on your fingertip so that you can secretly take pictures or shoot video. Imagine riding on the Uno, a speedy electric motorcycle that looks like a futuristic unicycle. And, if your head is spinning from thinking about all these imaginative gadgets, check out the Ostrich Pillow, which creates a cocoon for your head so you can nap whenever and wherever you want.

Be sure to keep a watch out for the book's special sections—7 Fantastic Finds for Food Fanatics and 7 Super High-Tech Gadgets—which show you what is possible, from printing your own sweet treats to answering phone calls from your glove. And wacky ideas aren't limited to today: You'll also find some harebrained ideas from history!

These amazing inventions are not only fun to read about, they also push the limits of technology. From boats that can drive to cars that can fly, you have to see them to believe them. So sit back—and prepare to be wowed!

CITYCAR FOLD-UP
VEHICLE, PAGE 58

FLY CITYCOPTER,
PAGE 54

LAND ROCKET

Imagine traveling **faster than the speed of sound. The Bloodhound SuperSonic Car (SSC)** will be the first car to attempt to break the **1,000-mile-an-hour (1,609-km/h) barrier.** (The current record is 763 miles an hour [1,228 km/h].) A concept for now, the rocket-shaped car gets its initial push to **350 miles an hour** (563 km/h) from a jet engine. Then a rocket fires up, blasting the SSC past 1,000 miles an hour. In order to keep the car streamlined, the driver lies back at a **45-degree angle** in a bathtub-shaped cockpit and navigates with controls that are a cross between those of a car and a jet. The SSC has three sets of brakes: flaps that rise from the body to create drag, **a parachute** that flies out of the back, and a set of wheel brakes to bring the car to a complete halt. So just what does it mean to be going 1,000 miles an hour? It's the same as shooting down four football fields in one second. **In other words, it's blink-of-an-eye fast.**

THE EMOTIV HEADSET

You're **playing a video game,** and all of a sudden you encounter a crate that needs to be moved. Instead of maneuvering a joystick, you think to yourself, "Push that crate." The crate amazingly shifts! The **Emotiv headset** is a helmet that uses **thought control** to interact with video games. **Sensors** in the helmet read the **electrical signals** in your **brain** to figure out what you're thinking. The helmet recognizes certain game-related actions, facial expressions, and even a few emotions. Be careful what you **think!**

1 THE CAR IS ABOUT AS LONG AS AN 18-WHEELER.

2 THE BLOODHOUND'S ENGINE IS SIX TIMES MORE POWERFUL THAN A RACE CAR'S.

3 A SONIC BOOM IS HEARD WHEN OBJECTS TRAVEL AT THE SPEED OF SOUND.

SURROUND SOUND

Talk about really tuning in. The **AudioOrb** truly lets you get into your favorite songs! Step into this **soundproof** Plexiglass **sphere** and become immersed in music, thanks to **18 speakers** that send sound waves around the orb. Just don't plan on having a dance party in there—the AudioOrb is equipped with a soft bench and comfy pillows, so you're meant to **sit back** and **relax** as you float away in your bubble of music.

ON A ROLL

Going somewhere? Try taking a turn inside this single-wheeled recreational vehicle. Measuring about 5.6 feet (1.7 m) in diameter, the Wheelsurf consists of two circular frames: The inner one holds the engine and seat; the outer one rotates around it. You use hand controls to speed up, slow down, and turn, but the real key to riding the Wheelsurf is to shift your body weight. Lean forward as you use the controls to accelerate and shift backward when you want to. Once you've got the hang of it, you can add to the thrill of riding by trying tricks such as somersaults or zipping round and round in tight circles. You're always on a roll while riding the Wheelsurf!

1 THE WHEELSURF CAN REACH SPEEDS OF 20 MILES AN HOUR (32 KM/H).

2 YOU START UP THE WHEELSURF BY PULLING A CHAIN ON THE MOTOR.

3 THE FIRST MONO-WHEEL WAS INVENTED IN 1869 IN FRANCE.

BOAT IN A BOX

This will totally **float your boat**. The Oru Kayak is a 12-foot (3.6-m)-long vessel that folds down into a carrying case that is **not much bigger** than a **pizza box**. What makes it so **portable**? The kayak's thin plastic frame contains several creases that allow you to bend it into a **compact** shape in about **five minutes**. The boat's seat cushion and footrest fit snugly into the Oru when it's in carrying-case mode. At just **25 pounds** (11.3 kg), it's probably the only boat you can fit inside your car!

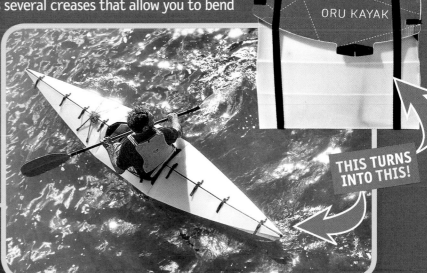

ORU KAYAK

THIS TURNS INTO THIS!

CARDBOARD BIKE

Here's a new twist on the idea of r*ecycling*: a cardboard bike! Phil Bridge, a design student in the United Kingdom, used **extra-thick** cardboard to create a bike frame complete with handlebars and a seat (the tires and chain are regular rubber and metal). The bike, which cost around **$25 to build,** can support a rider weighing up to about 170 pounds (77 kg)—and it's sturdy enough to leave out in the rain. And while it rides like a normal bike, it's definitely **not** speedy. As Bridge says, "It was designed for everyday use, so people riding it **slowly** to get from place to place, not the Tour de France!"

13

UNDERWATER WINGS

Ever wonder what it would feel like to glide through the ocean like a dolphin? With the **Subwing**, the experience is literally within your grasp. Made of lightweight, flexible **carbon fiber**, the Subwing acts like a fin that allows you to **slice through the water** in all different directions. The Subwing attaches to a boat and pulls you beneath the surface of the water. Tip the wings forward to **dive down**. Tilt the wings to one side and send yourself **spinning and spiraling** with the fish. Ready to come up for air? Point the Subwing toward the surface, and you'll be abovewater in seconds. Catch your breath, tighten your grip, and **dive back in again for more!**

1 AN ATTACHABLE LIGHT ON THE SUBWING LETS YOU EXPLORE AT NIGHT.

2 BOTTLENOSE DOLPHINS SURFACE TO BREATHE A FEW TIMES EACH MINUTE!

3 THE INVENTOR FIRST TESTED HIS IDEA BY HOLDING ON TO A PIECE OF DRIFTWOOD THAT WAS BEING TOWED BY A BOAT.

1 BUSINESS JETS FLY AT AROUND 50,000 FEET (15,240 M).

MARTIN JETPACK

2 THE INVENTOR HAS BEEN WORKING ON PERFECTING THE JETPACK FOR MORE THAN 30 YEARS.

3 THE JETPACK IS ABOUT AS TALL AS AN ASIAN ELEPHANT.

FLYING SOLO

You're **running late** to your cousin's birthday party, and you promised to arrive early to help set up. **There's no way** your bike is going to get you there **on time**, so instead you strap on your personal flying machine, elevate **straight up into the air**, and zip across town to land in your cousin's yard just in time. The **Martin Jetpack** is all about fun in the wild blue yonder. It flies you through the air at **highway speeds** (about 60 miles an hour [97 km/h]), traveling up to 30 miles (48 km) on a tank of gas. Driving it is like playing a video game—a **joystick-like handle** on the left moves you forward, back, left, and right, while another stick on the right sends you **up** and **down**. You fly about 500 feet (152 m) off of the ground, the height of a 50-story building. That's high enough to soar over trees and rooftops but still low enough to see all your jealous friends **gazing up at you in amazement**.

AIRLESS TIRES

Flat tires can totally **slow a driver down.** But some day in the not-so-distant future, we may never have to deal with that major drag. In years to come, cars could be outfitted with **airless tires,** which use slated plastic spokes instead of a cushion of air to **absorb shock.** The outside of these airless tires

would be coated with a **thin rubber tread** that can be replaced after it has been worn down. And because the entire thing would be recyclable, there won't be so many old tires filling up landfills like there are today. Now *that's* an idea **we can roll with.**

PALM TREE PHONE TOWER

That palm tree sure popped out of nowhere! But it's not a new type of tree that grows overnight; it's a cell phone tower in disguise. The camouflaged towers blend into the natural background and are meant to be easier on the eyes than the hulking utility poles that are needed to carry all of our cell phone calls. So you might spot a palm tree tower in the tropics, a cactus tower in the desert, or a Douglas fir tower in the mountains. But you won't likely find an oak tree tower anywhere: Because if there's one thing these towers can't do, it's get their leaves to change colors.

1 THE SKY-CAR COULD FLY OVER MOUNT EVEREST.

2 THE SKY-CAR WILL WEIGH ABOUT ABOUT THE SAME AS A GIRAFFE.

FLYING CARS!

Think about how awesome this would be: After school you ride your bike to the local verti-port (an airport designed for vertical takeoffs); tell a computer you're going to visit grandma, who lives 600 miles (966 km) away; and climb into a futuristic-looking car. The car rises into the air like a helicopter and then zooms ahead at 300 miles an hour (483 km/h), whisking you to grandma's house in two hours. Sounds like a vision for the year 2550, right? Well, this could happen in just ten years, according to Paul Moller, who invented the Skycar. And because the Skycar will be computerized, anyone—even kids—can drive it!

OUTDOOR GAMING

Who says you have to stay cooped up inside to play your favorite online game? In Paris, France, you can blend the best of both worlds with outdoor Play Tables. Using the city's free Wi-Fi, the touch-screen tables are like oversize iPads, offering free games from different designers. Adjust the angle of the screen to your liking, then sit down and play away. *Candy Crush Saga*, anyone?

INSTANT SEAT

It's always polite to offer visiting pals a place to sit, but what if you have more guests than seats? Pull out a spare chair! Developed by design students in Israel, the Foldigon is a small table that transforms into a comfy armchair in less than a minute. Plush fabric hidden inside the table unfolds and takes the shape of a chair. It's the perfect piece of furniture for anyone with a little space and a lot of friends.

QUICK CHANGE

1

PRINT YOUR OWN SWEETS

Satisfy your sweet tooth *stat* with the **ChefJet Pro 3-D food printer**. First, choose from **tasty flavors** such as **mint, milk chocolate, or sour cherry**. Next, pick your favorite design, hit print, and watch as special sugars work like **ink** to build up candies **layer by layer** right in front of your eyes. Recipes are sent straight to the printer using a **digital cookbook**, meaning you hardly have to lift a finger to create your confections.

7 FANTASTIC FINDS for FOOD FANATICS

2

PUSH FOR PIZZA

Your **belly is grumbling,** but the refrigerator is bare. **Don't panic!** Just **push the button** inside the box-shaped magnet on your fridge and—*mama mia!*—a piping-hot **pizza** arrives at your door in **30 minutes.** It might seem magical, but the **V.I.P. Fridge Magnet** actually contains a **transmitter** that places an order for your favorite pizza with just one touch. Right now, this amazing magnet is available only to customers of **Red Tomato Pizza** in the United Arab Emirates, but its inventors predict it will catch on elsewhere. Pizza party, anyone?

SING ALONG WITH YOUR SANDWICH

3

It's a **lunch box** ... it's a **music box** ... it's a **musical lunch box!** In 2012, a Portuguese company started selling "soundwiches": Sandwiches such as ham and cheese, smoked salmon, or turkey served in a metal lunch box (that you later return) that **plays a song** when you open it. Each sells for less than $10, meaning you pay only a small fee for lunch and a song!

INSTA-MEALS? 4
JUST PRESS PRINT

Forget the microwave. The **Foodini 3-D printer** may be your new **favorite kitchen gadget**. The machine quickly turns **fresh ingredients** into **complete dishes**. Perhaps the best part: Your favorite foods—nuggets, tiny quiches, crackers, chocolates—can be printed in **fun shapes** such as dinosaurs and snowmen.

NAPKIN TABLE

5

Bring lunch with a buddy to a new level with the **Napkin Table**. Designed with **friendship** in mind, the Napkin Table truly elevates your meal by **connecting you and your pal** as you picnic. Each of you slips the napkin straps around your neck, and then you balance the **portable, foldable** picnic table between the two of you. While stitched pockets and **cup holders** keep tableware in place, you still need to **stay in sync** with your chum while you chow so you don't tip your table. And, by keeping your food off the ground, you don't have to *bug* out about ants crawling all over your meal. **Bonus!**

INDOOR PICNIC

Planning a picnic is easy if you have a big backyard or live near a park. But what if the weather turns ugly, or you live in a city? Fortunately, you can bring the outdoors inside with the PicNYC table. Its aluminum frame and tabletop form a deep bed for growing a lush lawn that is the perfect setting for an urban picnic. You can even sprout an herb garden instead of grass. (Imagine plucking some fresh mint for your ice cream from the garden right next to your bowl!) Indoor picnickers may need coasters to stabilize their glasses in the thick grass—unless they're drinking water. In that case, a spill is actually good for the table!

7

SEE-THROUGH TOASTER

You've probably forgotten to adjust the toaster setting properly and ended up with burned toast that's hard enough to hammer nails. Or maybe your bread has popped up before it was barely brown at all. That's because English muffins, frozen waffles, bagels, and even different types of bread all have different moisture content and require different toaster settings. Get ready to say goodbye to still cold waffles and charred bagels forever. With the see-through toaster—just a concept for now—it's simple to watch what you're toasting turn the perfect shade of brown. It's the best thing since sliced bread.

THE SHIP CAN FLOAT 12,000 FEET (3,658 M) IN THE AIR.

1 «

THERE ARE ACCOMMODATIONS FOR ABOUT 120 PEOPLE ON BOARD.

2 «

THE AIRCRUISE TRAVELS AT AROUND 80 MILES AN HOUR (129 KM/H).

3 »

RAEMIAN
AIRCRUISE

来美安
RAEMIAN

HOTEL IN THE CLOUDS

The Aircruise is part blimp, part hotel, and totally cool. **This futuristic airship** is designed to float slowly through the sky. Passengers will board the Aircruise at special docking stations and cruise from New York City to London in 37 hours, or from Los Angeles to Shanghai, China, in 90 hours. Similar to a blimp, the Aircruise lifts into the air using **hydrogen gas.** Fuel cells and solar power run everything from lights and TVs to the ship itself while the Aircruise is aloft. Nearly as **tall as the Eiffel Tower,** the ship has plenty of room to roam, with ten apartments, an open-air deck, massive dining and recreation areas, and—at the very bottom—a lounge with a **glass floor** where you can watch birds fly *beneath* you.

MOW-BOT

Mowing the lawn is a sweaty way to spend a Saturday afternoon. Imagine if you could get the job done with the **flip of a switch**. Once charged and activated, an electric robot called the **Automower** quietly trundles across the lawn and cuts the grass. It **senses obstacles automatically** by gently bumping into them and stays within the boundaries of your yard through electronic signals transmitted by wires buried under the grass. The mower operates **rain or shine** and will even send a **text message** to you if it gets into trouble. When the battery is low, the Automower returns to its **recharging station** for a refresher before heading back out to finish the job.

FACE-MASK CAMERA

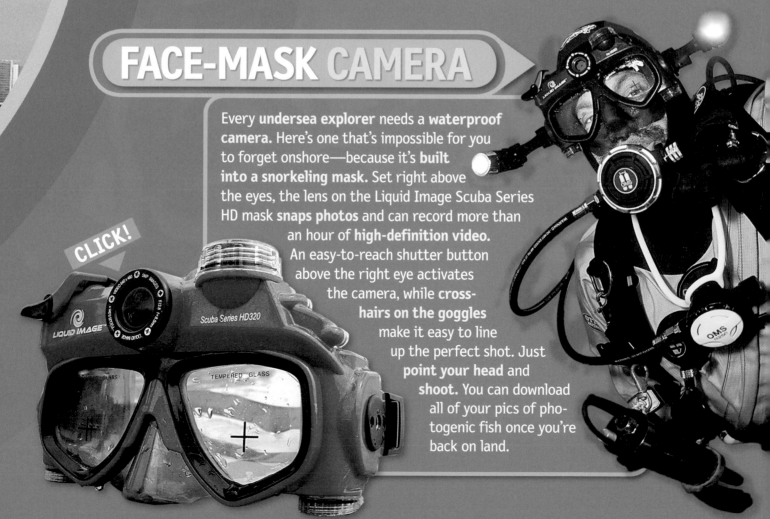

Every **undersea explorer** needs a **waterproof camera**. Here's one that's impossible for you to forget onshore—because it's **built into a snorkeling mask**. Set right above the eyes, the lens on the Liquid Image Scuba Series HD mask **snaps photos** and can record more than an hour of **high-definition video**. An easy-to-reach shutter button above the right eye activates the camera, while **crosshairs on the goggles** make it easy to line up the perfect shot. Just **point your head** and **shoot.** You can download all of your pics of photogenic fish once you're back on land.

CLICK!

THE FIRST GYROPLANE WAS INVENTED MORE THAN 90 YEARS AGO.

1 «

YOU HAVE TO HAVE A PILOT'S LICENSE TO FLY THE SUPER SKY CYCLE.

2 «

YOU CAN FILL UP THE SUPER SKY CYCLE AT YOUR LOCAL GAS STATION.

3

EXPERIME

FLYING MOTORCYCLE

We may not have flying cars **yet**, but here's the next best thing: **a flying motorcycle!** This three-wheeled vehicle really reaches new heights when its rotor blades (similar to a helicopter's) start spinning. On just one tank of gas, the **Super Sky Cycle** can **fly for hours** at speeds up to **100 miles an hour** (160 km/h). If the engine loses power, its unpowered top rotor is even more effective than a parachute, allowing you to float down to the ground. Want to hit the road? Fold down the blades, and you can **cruise in the cycle as fast as a car** on a highway. And at under eight feet (2.4 m) tall, you can easily park it in your garage!

BIG SCREENS FOR BACKYARDS

If you want **extreme pool-party fun**, you can float while enjoying **big entertainment**. The inflatable **SuperScreen Mini in a Box** provides a movie theater—like experience in your own backyard. The **7-foot (2.1-m)-tall, 12-foot (3.7-m)-wide screen** is **flexible**, like a piece of cloth, and zips into an inflatable frame. All you do is attach a **blower** and watch it inflate like a big **balloon**. Straps let you tie the SuperScreen to trees or secure it to hooks in the ground so it won't blow away. Also included are a **DVD player**, **projector**, and **speakers**. The pool is optional.

SOLAR-POWERED TENT

Oh no! You're camping with your family, and your iPod battery just drained. Normally you would be out of luck, but this time you're sleeping in a **Bang Bang solar-powered tent**. This brightly colored four-person tent comes equipped with a **solar panel** that soaks up sunlight all day. This creates enough energy to charge a lithium battery bank inside the tent. So all you have to do is **connect your gadget** to a USB adapter attached to the battery bank and charge away. Now you'll always have enough juice in your iPod to have that **dance party under the stars**.

CAR + PLANE

If a long road trip sounds boring, the Transition is for you. It's a car that turns into a plane! You can drive the Transition to the local airport, press a button, and transform the vehicle from an automobile to an airplane. Watch the rear bumper fold down and the wings unfurl from the sides like a bird's wings. Thirty seconds later, the Transition is ready to take flight. It can fly about 120 miles an hour (193 km/h) at an altitude of about a mile (1.6 km). (Commercial jets cruise far higher—about seven miles [11.3 km] up.) Think about it: A trip that would ordinarily have taken five hours in a car will take under two hours in the Transition. Go ahead, wave sympathetically to all those people stuck in traffic beneath you.

MUSICAL DOG

I-Dog is one canine with rhythm! Sit this robot pup in front of some tunes—or hook it up to an MP3 player—and it starts grooving to the music by moving its head and wriggling its ears. Lights on its face flash to the beat in various colors that represent how I-Dog feels about different types of music. Play rock and I-Dog might light up red; with hip-hop it may turn yellow. There's trouble, however, if I-Dog's middle light blinks purple. That means your pal is in need of some loving. Luckily I-Dog is easy to perk up. Just keep playing music and press the button on its face, or "pet" it by waving your hand over its head. I-Dog will be dancing again in no time.

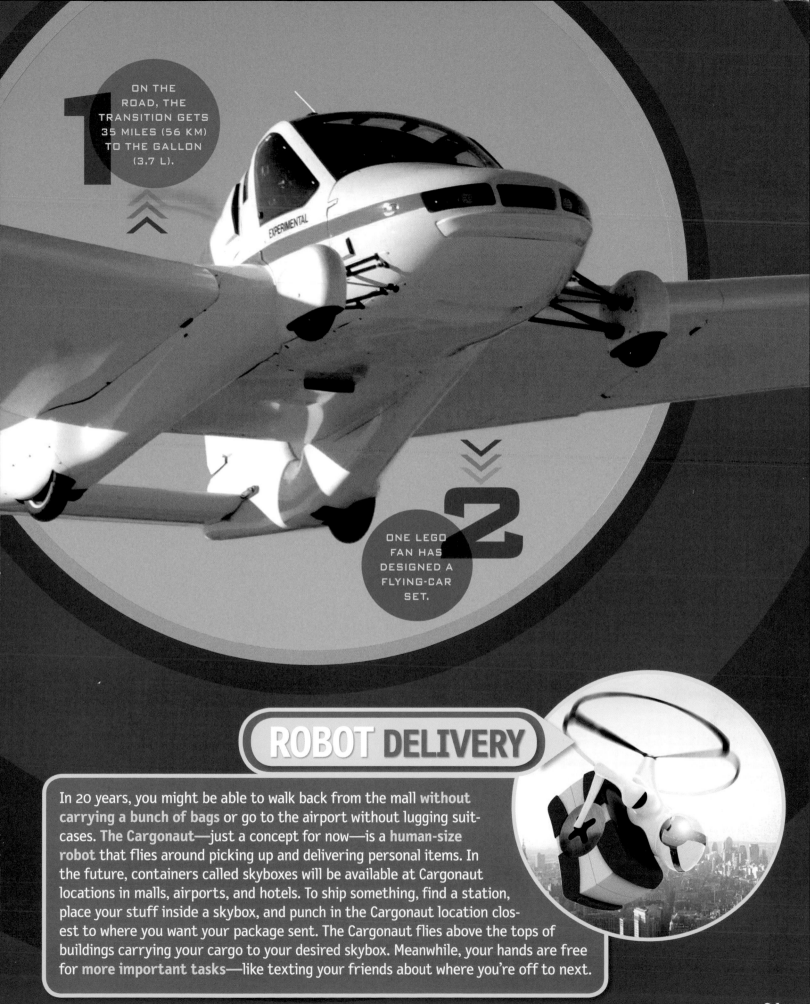

1 ON THE ROAD, THE TRANSITION GETS 35 MILES (56 KM) TO THE GALLON (3.7 L).

2 ONE LEGO FAN HAS DESIGNED A FLYING-CAR SET.

ROBOT DELIVERY

In 20 years, you might be able to walk back from the mall **without carrying a bunch of bags** or go to the airport without lugging suitcases. **The Cargonaut**—just a concept for now—is a **human-size robot** that flies around picking up and delivering personal items. In the future, containers called skyboxes will be available at Cargonaut locations in malls, airports, and hotels. To ship something, find a station, place your stuff inside a skybox, and punch in the Cargonaut location closest to where you want your package sent. The Cargonaut flies above the tops of buildings carrying your cargo to your desired skybox. Meanwhile, your hands are free for **more important tasks**—like texting your friends about where you're off to next.

LIGHT-UP MOTORCYCLE

1 THE LIGHT CYCLE WAS INSPIRED BY A SIMILAR BIKE IN THE MOVIE *TRON: LEGACY*.

Most **sci-fi** movie vehicles are created on a computer and exist only on screen. But after seeing the **motorcycle** in the movie *TRON: Legacy,* a few inventors decided to turn that futuristic bike into reality with the **Light Cycle.** The blue lights lining the tires and body are actually sticker-like strips that have a special coating to make them **glow.** The Light Cycle's most distinctive feature is its hollow, **SUV-size** wheels. The bike's controls are like those on a regular motorcycle, but to drive it, you **lie on your stomach** and steer with your arms. Marc Parker, one of the bike's creators, says that the funky body position adds to the **thrill of the ride.** "You feel like Superman—like you're **flying.**"

2 THE BIKE IS ABOUT AS LONG AS A SMART CAR.

3 THE LIGHT CYCLE'S CREATORS HAVE ALSO MADE A REPLICA OF THE BATMOBILE.

DOOR BECOMES GAME

The knocking on this door isn't from guests—it's the sound of **bouncing Ping-Pong balls.** The Ping-Pong Door transforms from a door to a **table tennis court** in three seconds. Just push the top of the door's built-in panel to unlock it, and then **swing the panel** into a horizontal position to get your game on. Once you're finished playing, push the panel back up into **door mode.** Both fun and functional, this invention deserves **big points.**

ROLLING ROBOT

Have you ever wanted to control your very own **robot** with your **smartphone?** Meet **Ollie,** a rolling orb that you can send spinning in any direction via a downloadable app on your phone. Equipped with **nubby tires,** this **rugged** robot—which is smaller than a soda can—rolls faster than you can ride your bike. Ollie can motor its way up and down hills and even along sandy stretches. Take it to the **skate park** and watch it catch major air and show off some sick **tricks** (Ollie is named after a skateboarding stunt, after all). If only it could teach you how to **pop a wheelie,** too!

1 REAL DOLPHINS CAN JUMP UP TO 20 FEET (6 M) IN THE AIR.

2 A VIDEO CAMERA MOUNTED TO THE DORSAL FIN LETS THE PILOT SEE WHAT'S GOING ON ABOVE THE SURFACE.

3 YOU CAN DO 360-DEGREE ROLLS WHILE TRAVELING ALONG THE SURFACE OF THE WATER.

DOLPHIN-SHAPED DIVING MACHINE

DRIVER'S SEAT

You'll definitely make waves riding in this water vehicle. The Seabreacher J is a **dolphin-shaped submersible** that can plunge 5 feet (1.5 m) deep, leap up to 12 feet (3.7 m) in the air, and skim along the water's surface at **50 miles an hour** (80 km/h). Pilot and passenger are strapped into a **watertight cockpit** complete with a stereo system and **GPS navigation**. Hand levers control the side fins while foot pedals move the tail. If **built-in sensors** detect that you've dived too deep, the engine turns off and the craft bobs to the surface. You can even get the Seabreacher J painted in colors of your choice so you can swish through the sea **in style**.

1 «««

ON THE GROUND AND IN THE SKY THE PAL-V CAN REACH 112 MILES AN HOUR (180 KM/H).

2 ⌄⌄

THE PAL-V CAN FLY AS HIGH AS 4,000 FEET (1,219 M).

3 «

IT TAKES ABOUT TEN MINUTES TO CONVERT FROM CAR TO PLANE.

SKY CAR

Sitting in bumper-to-bumper traffic is no fun. Too bad flying cars don't exist, right? Not quite. A prototype aircraft called the PAL-V (short for "personal air and land vehicle") transforms in about ten minutes from a three-wheeled roadster into a soaring gyrocopter—a sort of plane/helicopter hybrid. Fueled by regular gasoline, the PAL-V handles like a sports car on the ground but can also fly above jammed highways and over mountains with its pilot and one passenger. As the rotor blades rise, a push of a button extends the tail, readying the vehicle for flight. Because it's a gyrocopter, the PAL-V needs a runway to take off and land. Just hope you don't run into traffic on the way to the airport.

CAPTURING THE MOMENT

With a satisfying *thwack*, the ball soars off your bat and over the left-field fence. By the time you touch home plate, your brother, who's sitting in the stands, has **sent a video** of your awesome home run **across the country** to your grandparents. **The Looxcie** video camera perches on his ear, constantly capturing the action in front of him. When **something memorable happens**, he presses a button that automatically saves the **last 30 seconds** of video. He can share the clip on YouTube, Facebook, Twitter, or in an email. Now your friends will *have* to believe your story of hitting the **game-winning run.**

MOVABLE HOUSE

Want to live next door to your best friend? Just **move your house! The Walking House** is an agile abode that is about the size of a large room, with a bed and a small sitting area. It walks at human speeds but in a **buglike** fashion, using its **six legs** to maneuver in every direction. The Walking House's power comes straight from the sun—**solar panels** on the roof catch the rays needed to keep the house chugging along. A wood-burning stove, rainwater-catching system, and composting toilet keep things **eco-friendly.** The house is controlled by a computer and **GPS,** a technology that uses satellites to figure out the dwelling's current location. Whenever you feel like moving, just punch in **where you want to go** and satellites will guide the house to your destination. Making your best friend your neighbor is a breeze!

ABOARD PHYSALIA

RIVER-CLEANING BOAT

It may float, but this is not your ordinary boat. The **translucent, curvy** *Physalia* (just a concept now) is a **floating museum** and **research lab**. Its mission: to make the planet greener. How? As it glides down a dirty river, the river water is pumped to *Physalia*'s **rooftop garden**; plants **filter** and **purify** water, which then flows back into the river. The boat powers itself; solar panels on top capture energy from the sun, while **hydroturbines** underneath convert moving water into **electricity**. As the boat's scientists study the river's ecosystem, visitors hop aboard to view exhibits and relax.

ONCE BUILT, THE BOAT SHOULD CREATE MORE ENERGY THAN IT CONSUMES.

DID YOU KNOW? ABOUT ONE IN EIGHT PEOPLE CURRENTLY LACKS ACCESS TO SAFE WATER SUPPLIES.

THE BOAT'S DESIGN WAS INSPIRED BY THE JELLYFISH-LIKE PORTUGUESE MAN-OF-WAR, ALSO KNOWN AS *PHYSALIA PHYSALIS*.

THE ROOF OPENS

ROVING RESIDENCE

You're in the middle of a bike ride when your stomach starts growling. Luckily you brought your kitchen—and your living room and bedroom—along for the ride. The Tricycle House is a plastic pod that fits on the back of an adult-size tricycle. It offers most of the comforts of home thanks to convertible furniture and hidden compartments. For instance, the table transforms into a bed or shelving. A sink, bathtub, and electric stove all unfold from the walls, which are designed to let sunlight in during the day and streetlamp light at night. Multiple Tricycle Houses can even be linked together to create a palace in any parking lot.

A REALLY ROCKING CHAIR

The iRock definitely isn't your grandma's rocking chair! In this wooden chair, equipped with a built-in iPad dock and speakers, you can rock out while you, um, *rock*. The iRock harvests the energy from your movement to power your iPhone or iPad. In fact, an hour of rocking will recharge your gadget's battery to about 35 percent. Now that's a concept worth sitting down for.

BUILT-IN SPEAKERS

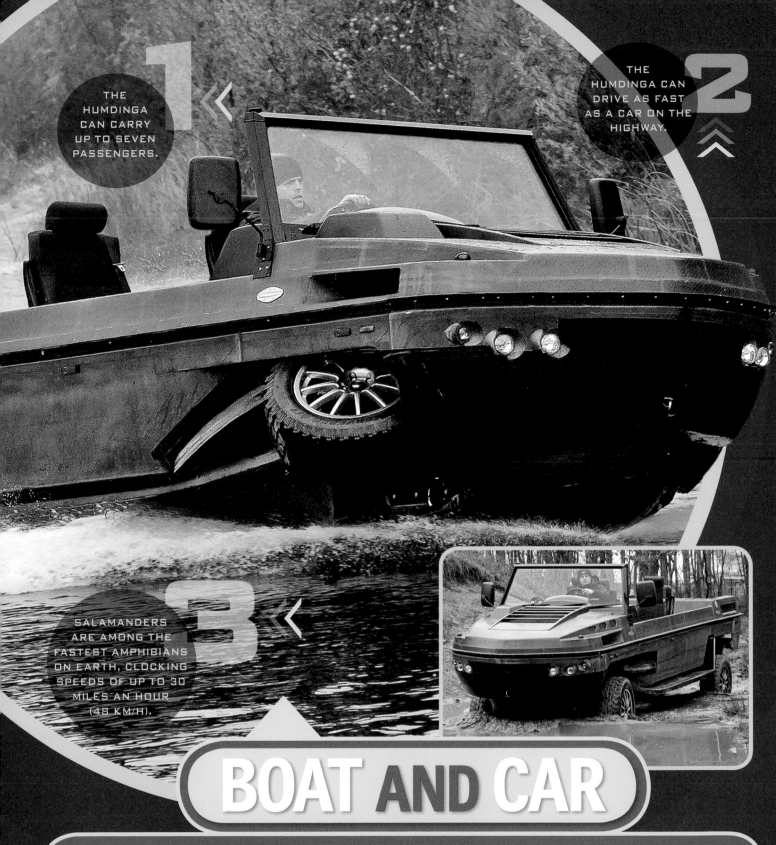

1 THE HUMDINGA CAN CARRY UP TO SEVEN PASSENGERS.

2 THE HUMDINGA CAN DRIVE AS FAST AS A CAR ON THE HIGHWAY.

3 SALAMANDERS ARE AMONG THE FASTEST AMPHIBIANS ON EARTH, CLOCKING SPEEDS OF UP TO 30 MILES AN HOUR (48 KM/H).

BOAT AND CAR

The Humdinga is a vehicle that knows how to make a splash. This **amphibious truck turned boat** drives on land and in water. But unlike similar vehicles, the Humdinga can **lift its wheels completely** out of the water, allowing it to sail through waves at **high speeds**. Going from street to surf is easy—just drive it down a ramp or beach until the wheels are **submerged**, and then **press a button** to fold up the wheels. **Now it's a boat.** The Humdinga is designed for disaster relief, such as bringing supplies to flood zones. But it also can be used for fun. Picture yourself driving along the streets of San Francisco, California, U.S.A., and then straight into the city's bay for a lap around Alcatraz Island. Now that's the way to **go sightseeing.**

1
THE SPNKIX RUBBER WHEELS ARE ABOUT THE SIZE OF A BAGEL.

MOTORIZED SKATES

It'd be awesome to cruise along on roller skates without ever having to push off. With spnKiX (pronounced "spin kicks"), you can do just that. These accelerating accessories are like small motorized vehicles that you strap to your shoes. Each spnKiX skate has a tiny electric motor that can propel the skater up to ten miles an hour (16 km/h)—about as fast as a swift jogger—for about six miles (10 km) on one battery charge. The rider controls the speed with a wireless handheld remote and skids to a stop using heel brakes. But just because the skates are motorized doesn't mean you get a free ride. "You need to use muscles to balance and steer," spnKiX inventor Peter Treadway says. "You'll still sweat."

3
ROLLER SKATES HAVE BEEN AROUND SINCE THE EARLY 18TH CENTURY (BUT NOT LIKE THIS!).

OPEN

FOLDING BATHTUB

Just because you have a **small bathroom** doesn't mean you can't have a tub. Designed for bathrooms with **limited space**, the Tulip is a concept that **converts** a shower into a bathtub. Rough day at soccer practice? Simply pull down on the front to open the tub, **fill it with water**, and slip under the suds. A wireless **touchscreen** panel lets you control underwater jets to massage your sorest muscles. *Ahh … now that's* **relaxing!**

CLOSED

SPNKIX CAN ROLL FOR 40 MINUTES ON A SINGLE CHARGE.

2

SOLAR PANEL

POWER PACK

Uh-oh! Your smartphone is **about to die**, but you left your **charger** at home. No need to panic if you have the **A-Solar Nova Backpack**: This knapsack is also a charger! Its built-in solar panel soaks up the **sun**, using energy from the rays to charge a small **internal battery** in about ten hours. (Plug the battery directly into a wall outlet to charge it faster.) Once the battery is fully juiced, connect your **gadgets** to it with cords inside the carrier. You can recharge all of your **small electronics**, including smartphones, portable game systems, and music players—which all fit nicely into the backpack's **padded pockets.**

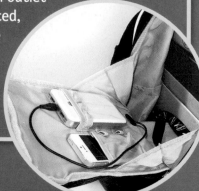

MOBILE HOTEL ROOM

You love the idea of **sleeping under the stars.** But sleeping on the ground? Not so much. Enter the **Travelpod,** a mobile hotel room that lets you **enjoy camping** without having to really rough it. Housed in a clear **plexiglass box** that's about the size of your bedroom, the Travelpod offers all of the luxuries of a hotel room smack in the middle of the wilderness: a double bed with **fluffy pillows, a desk, a carpeted floor,** and a **private bathroom.** The pod even has its own generator so you can have lights or power up your gadgets. Ready for bed? **Pull the curtains** tight and hit the hay. Sure brings new meaning to the *great* outdoors!

OSTRICH PILLOW

Sometimes traveling makes you want to **bury your head in the sand.** That's where the **Ostrich Pillow** can come in handy. Stay comfy, hide from the world, and catch some **z's** anywhere you want with this **portable pillow.** Just slip it over your head, making sure the big opening is over your mouth so you can breathe easily (there are two other holes to stick your hands in as you sleep). Then **rest your head** wherever you can, like on a table or desk, or on your big brother's shoulder as you ride in the car. The soft, cushioned interior makes even the hardest surface a **lovely place** to power nap.

1 THE BIKE WAS TESTED ON MOUNT SNOWDON, THE HIGHEST MOUNTAIN IN WALES.

2 A MAN ONCE CYCLED OVER 280 MILES (451 KM) IN 24 HOURS ON A MOUNTAIN BIKE.

3 CYCLISTS MUST REACH THE TOP OF THE HILL BY CAR OR GONDOLA BEFORE RIDING DOWN.

4-WHEELED MOUNTAIN BIKE

When Calvin Williams injured his legs from a fall off a cliff, he spent a year **recovering in a wheelchair**. Soon Williams, an engineering professor in Wales, U.K., began missing the **thrill of biking**, so he designed a **four-wheeled mountain bike** specifically for **disabled riders**. Super-lightweight—and superfast—the **Project Enduro** bike uses suspension technology similar to that used in a **Formula 1 race car**. While the bike lacks pedals and is only good for downhill trails, it still offers the thrill of cycling.

ELECTRIC TRICYCLE

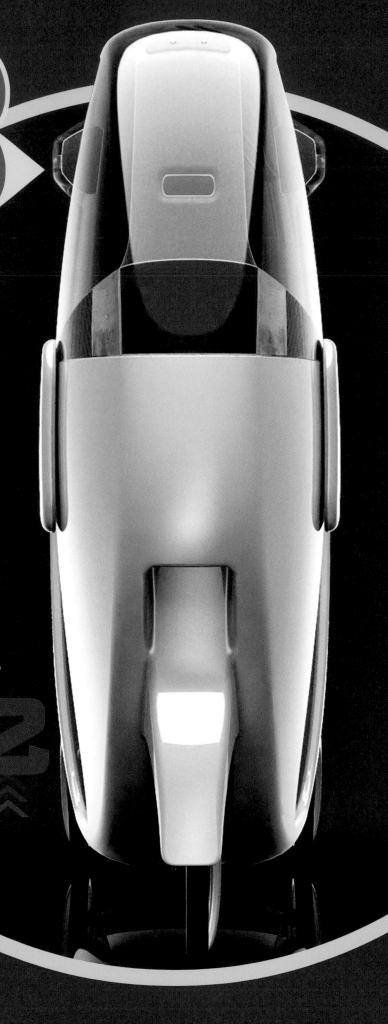

Imagine if your **bicycle** had all the features of a **car**, right down to a windshield wiper, a trunk for stashing your stuff, and even a **motor**. The **Emcycle** encloses the rider in a rain-shielding shell complete with **locking doors** and **three** wheels so it won't topple over at stop signs. As with a bicycle, **you pedal** the Emcycle and steer it with handlebars. But pedaling also charges an **electric motor** that boosts your speed up to **40 miles an hour (64 km/h)**. "That makes you feel like Superman—it amplifies your pedal power **two to three times**," inventor Michael Scholey says. A dashboard on the handlebars features **battery** and **speed** displays, plus controls for the turn signals, heater, and headlights. You can even add a radio and a cup holder. Talk about a **sweet ride!**

1 ❮❮❮ THE EMCYCLE CAN CARRY A DRIVER AND UP TO 75 POUNDS (34 KG) OF LUGGAGE.

2 ❮❮ THE TRIKE'S NO-PUNCTURE TIRES ARE FILLED WITH FOAM.

MOBILE SAUNA

Want to get your steam on in the snow? With this sauna on wheels, that's no problem. Big enough to fit more than one person, the sauna is towed around by a bike to wherever you want—in any type of temperature. Even if it's freezing outside, the sauna stays toasty warm with a wood-burning fire-place and an elastic cover to keep it a balmy 180°F (80°C). That's hotter than the Sahara!

THE INVENTOR ALSO DESIGNS HOT WHEELS CARS.

>> 3

ENERGY TRACKER

The Vigo wants to make sure you never snooze in school again. By tracking your alertness, this digital device "nudges" you when it's time to wake up. How? Using a motion sensor, the Vigo— which you wear over your ear like a Bluetooth headset—tracks how much you blink and your body movements to determine if you're losing steam. When it detects that you're drowsy, you get an alert that prompts you to perk up. What kind of alert you receive is up to you: Set the Vigo to vibrate your phone, play your favorite pump-up song, or illuminate an LED notification light. Use whatever it takes to wake you up—and get you totally tuned in to your teacher.

7 SUPER-HIGH-Tech GADGETS

1

FINGERTIP CAMERA

Measuring about an inch on all sides, the **world's smallest camera** is slightly larger than a piece of bubble gum. The camera has a single **button on top** that lets you switch between **taking photos** and **recording videos**. A strap allows you to tote it on your keychain, backpack, or wrist, so you can shoot wherever you are. You can **aim the lens** between the bars of your guinea pig's cage, pop it around the corner to snap **surprise shots** of your friends at school, or hide it while you take **secret footage** of your brother's self-proclaimed "awesome" dance moves. (Maybe if he actually *sees* himself ...)

2

GLOVE MAKES CALLS

This is one *handy* smartphone accessory. Artist Sean Miles invented a glove with a **built-in microphone** and **speaker** that connects to any standard smartphone that has a **wireless Bluetooth** signal. Just slip on the glove and make or answer a call on your phone. After tucking the mobile device away, **speak into the glove's pinkie and listen through its thumb.** Miles designed the glove to promote recycling—all of the stylish accessory's electronic parts come from old mobile devices. This gives new meaning to "Talk to the hand!"

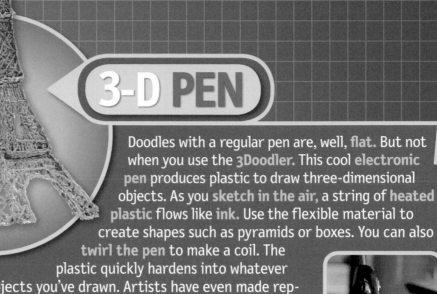

3-D PEN

3

Doodles with a regular pen are, well, **flat.** But not when you use the 3Doodler. This cool **electronic pen** produces plastic to draw three-dimensional objects. As you **sketch in the air,** a string of **heated plastic** flows like **ink.** Use the flexible material to create shapes such as pyramids or boxes. You can also **twirl the pen** to make a coil. The plastic quickly hardens into whatever objects you've drawn. Artists have even made replicas of the Eiffel Tower (left) and model dinosaurs with the pen. Just **pick a good spot** to display your doodle masterpieces—these drawings definitely won't fit on the pages of your notebook.

4

SMART RING

Picture this: You're sitting on the couch watching your favorite TV show and you want to **turn the volume up.** No need to grab the remote: Just tap your thumb to your ring finger to increase the sound. And while you're at it, **make a call,** too—all without even touching your phone. That's what **Fin,** a smart ring, can do. Just slide the ring onto your thumb and it uses a Bluetooth sensor and **gesture-recognition** technology to control your smart devices wirelessly. **Sync it** to your smart gadget and you can call a friend or **shoot off a text** just by moving your thumb over your other fingers. This ring's not quite a magic wand—but it's just about the **next best thing.**

7 SUPER-HIGH-TECH GADGETS

5 GOOGLE GLASS

Have you ever seen someone **walk into a wall** while reading a text message? Maybe that someone was you? **Google Glass**, an eyeglass frame developed by **Google**, can help phone fanatics avoid such embarrassing mishaps. Think of it as a **smartphone for your eyeballs**. The frame's eyepiece displays all sorts of **handy data**—from texts to your calendar. Lost? Just ask the **voice-activated** display for directions and it'll **project a map** to your destination. See something cool? Tell Google Glass to **take a picture**—or even a video—and then **share** the scene with your friends as you chat with them on the **built-in phone**. Whatever you see, they see. Just watch out for walls.

6 LIGHT-UP GLOVES

These gloves put safety right in your own hands. Whether you're biking, running, or skateboarding down the street, these gloves will **keep you safe** and seen even if you're out and about after the sun goes down. Just touch your thumb and index finger together to activate bright **LED lights** that act as **turn signals**. And no sweat if you forget to charge them up: The gloves' superefficient battery gets you **two months** of daily blinking. What a *bright* idea!

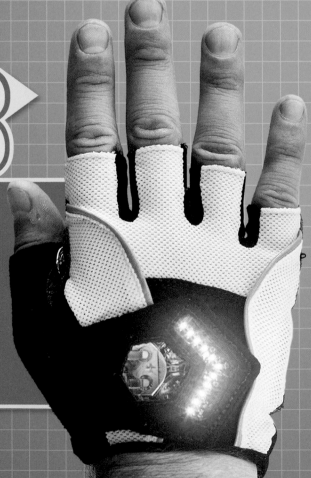

INFLATABLE BIKE HELMET

See ya, helmet head. With an inflatable bike helmet, your do stays put—and you stay safe at the same time. Worn like a collar around your neck, this high-tech helmet inflates within one-tenth of a second if it detects a crash (similar to how air bags work in a car). Made of nylon fabric, the collar quickly fills with helium, enveloping your head with a protective hood before you hit the ground. That's one way to use your noodle while you ride your bike.

1

PERSONAL HELICOPTER

Imagine **never having to worry** about running **late** for school again. That would be the case if you had your own **Fly Citycopter**, a personal helicopter that **flies itself.** The futuristic concept of a Brazilian visual artist, the Fly Citycopter can take off, fly, and land while in **autopilot** mode. No need to worry about stopping for gas: The copter is designed to run on solar power and even generate energy, so it can fly for up to **300 miles (483 km).** And with the ability to reach speeds topping **100 miles an hour** (160 km/h), getting to school before the bell rings will be a breeze.

2

IT IS ABOUT THE SAME SIZE AS A CAR, BOTH IN LENGTH AND WEIGHT.

THE INTERIOR IS EQUIPPED WITH A JOYSTICK CONTROLLER AND TOUCH-SCREEN DIGITAL PANELS.

3

FLOATING VACATION

From a **shiplike hotel** to a **research station** for studying ocean animals, the **Utopia** can be many things—but it's mostly just **cool**. Just a concept for now, this large floating world rests on **four legs that extend** and float about **50 feet (15 m) below the surface**. These legs help minimize how much of the vessel actually touches the water, reducing movement caused by waves. When it's not a home for **marine biologists**, Utopia accommodates tourists, who travel there via **helicopter, boat,** or **mini-submarine** and lounge in luxurious guest suites, pools, and restaurants. There's even a movie theater. But the best part is the top deck, where a **360-degree observatory** high above the water's surface makes you feel as if you're on top of the world.

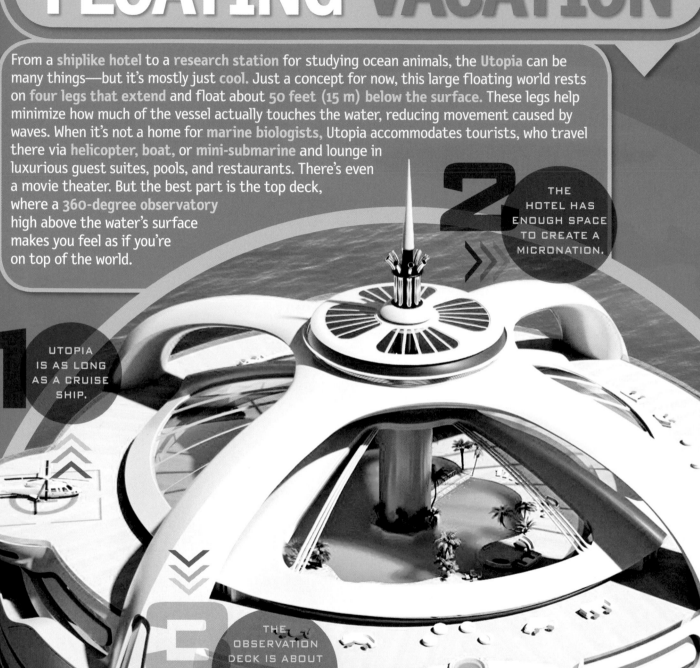

1 UTOPIA IS AS LONG AS A CRUISE SHIP.

2 THE HOTEL HAS ENOUGH SPACE TO CREATE A MICRONATION.

3 THE OBSERVATION DECK IS ABOUT 20 STORIES ABOVE THE WAVES.

LIGHT-UP FAUCET

Get a **light show** every time you brush your teeth or wash your hands with this **flashy faucet.** Turn off the lights and watch water spill out in **different colors** thanks to **temperature-sensitive,** built-in **LED lights.** Cool water flows **violet,** warm glows **green,** and hot water runs **red.** And with its sleek chrome finish, it looks like a **faucet from the future.** Washing up has never been such an *illuminating* experience!

BALL CAMERA

The **Panono Camera** really gets the **big picture.** The surface of the ball-shaped camera is embedded with **36 tiny cameras** that snap simultaneously to create a 360-degree panoramic image. **Chuck the Panono** into the air and the cameras **automatically** capture what's happening in all directions. Upload the images to your smartphone, tablet, or computer and a software program **weaves together** all of the photos to make one big image. Small and lightweight, the Panono can go just about anywhere. And the invention is **tough enough** to survive a drop if you don't catch it on the way down. **Heads up!**

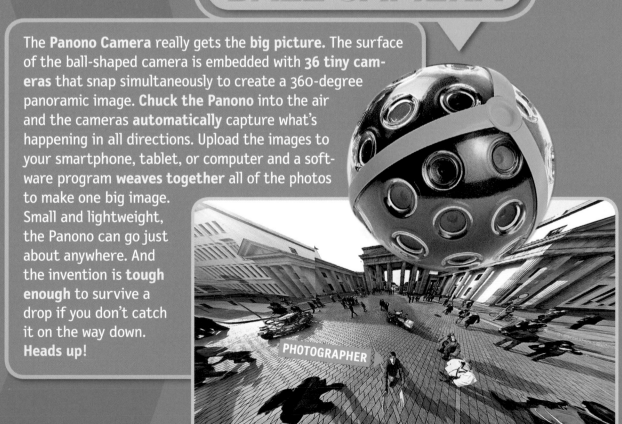

PHOTOGRAPHER

FOLD-UP CAR

Pulling up to your favorite restaurant for dinner, you see that cars parked along the curb **haven't left enough space** for a regular car to fit in. Luckily you have a **CityCar**. This prototype **fold-up vehicle** may help drivers slip into **tight spots** and replace bigger cars that crowd cities. The **electric** two-seater features an oval pod that fits a driver and one passenger. With the press of a button, the front and rear wheels **slide toward each other**, pushing the pod vertically. Folded, the Transformer-like car is **five feet** (1.5 m) long. (Most other cars stretch 16 feet [5 m].) With its tiny, flexible frame, the CityCar saves space, fuel—*and* your dinner plans.

THE CAR HAS NO DOORS; YOU ENTER THROUGH THE WINDSHIELD.

CITYCARS ARE STACKABLE.

1

2

THREE CITYCARS CAN FIT INTO ONE PARKING SPACE.

3

CHARGING TREE

Charge your iPod in an **environmentally friendly** way. Inspired by a **bonsai** tree, the Electree has branches with **solar panels** for "leaves." Position the tree however you like, designing different shapes and **angles** by rotating and moving the branches. Then just place it next to a window so the solar panels can **soak up** some rays. The energy produced by the panels is stored in a **battery** hidden in the base. When your phone, iPod, or DS starts running low on power, simply **plug it into the tree** to charge it. Now all you need is sunny weather.

BOARDING
WITHOUT LIMITS

Winter, spring, summer, fall—who cares what season it is? Surf, skate, and snowboard **all year long. The Human Touch iJoy Board** simulates the movement of all three sports. Using all of your muscles, you **balance** atop the motorized board as it pitches and rolls back and forth, side to side, and up and down. **Press a button** on the remote control to start it up and choose slow, medium, fast, or a mix of all three. **Just think** how prepared you'll be the next time you face a half-pipe or some **killer waves!**

JET-POWERED SURFBOARD

Surf's up! But the big waves are crashing so far away from the shore. No need to exhaust yourself paddling out to the them; just hop on a WaveJet, a jet-propelled surfboard, and you can reach the swells without breaking a sweat. Powered by a pair of battery-operated engines in a pod at the base of the board, you simply hit a switch on a wristband to pick your speed up to ten miles an hour (16 km/h), which is about five times the average person's paddling speed. Not a surfer? The removable engine pod can be attached to stand-up paddleboards, boogie boards, and kayaks, so you'll get a boost however you hit the water.

"SUN" GLASSES

Sometimes **gloomy winter weather** can make you feel, well, gloomy. But if you pop on these **glasses**, even the dreariest days will seem **sunny**. A team of engineers created these special glasses using **six LEDs** to create constant light for whoever wears them. A **reflector** on the glasses safely bounces the light around the eyes without blocking your vision. Experts say this kind of **constant light** can increase your energy levels and even combat **seasonal depression**. Bad moods, be gone!

3

THE BIGGEST WAVE EVER SURFED WAS ESTIMATED TO BE 80 FEET (24 M) TALL.

TINY TRANSMITTER!

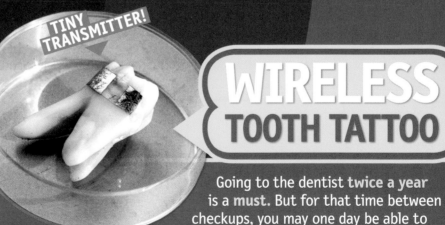

WIRELESS TOOTH TATTOO

Going to the dentist **twice a year** is a **must**. But for that time between checkups, you may one day be able to **keep tabs on your teeth** with a **wireless tooth tattoo**. Made of silk strands pulled from cocoons and gold wires skinnier than a spiderweb, this **tiny sensor** attaches to your tooth like a temporary tattoo. There, it **detects decay** or **harmful bacteria** brewing among your chompers. And if the tattoo senses something's amiss in your mouth, you'll get an alert on a handheld digital device. While scientists have **only tested** the tattoo on cows' teeth, they're hoping that one day the tattoo will **help humans** take a *bite* out of tooth decay for good.

PHONE-CHARGING BOOTS

You **just saw** an **awesome movie** and have *got* to call your best friend to gab about it. But as you're walking home from the theater, you realize your phone is dead. So you **slip it into your boot** and **walk faster.** That's the concept behind the **Orange Power Wellies:** boots that can **charge your phone.** Your feet produce heat as you walk, and a **thermoelectric** module in the boot's sole uses the difference in temperature between your feet and the cold ground to create electricity. The warmer your feet and the chillier the ground, the **more power** you produce. So keep walking—it'll keep **you** *and* **your phone** going.

VIRTUAL KEYBOARD

Tap out an **email right on** your **kitchen table** or type up a report on your bedroom floor. With the **Magic Cube,** you can turn any flat, opaque surface into a **keyboard.** Connect the small, cube-shaped device to a smartphone, tablet, or computer. The cube uses a laser beam to **project a keyboard** onto the surface. A **sensor** inside the cube **tracks** where your fingers are tapping and then translates the movements into letters and numbers. The cube even plays **tapping sounds** while you type, just in case you miss the **clickety-clack** of your old-fashioned keyboard.

THE SUCTION CAN STICK ONTO ANY BUILDING SURFACE, SUCH AS GLASS, STUCCO, OR BRICK.

1

HIBIKI GOT AN A ON HIS CLASS PROJECT.

2

DID YOU KNOW? SPIDERS HAVE TINY CLAWS ON THE TIPS OF THEIR LEGS THAT CLING TO SURFACES AND HELP THEM CLIMB UP TREES AND WALLS.

3

WALL WALKER

It took a **radioactive arachnid's bite** to turn Peter Parker into Spider-Man, but a schoolboy in the United Kingdom has devised an easier way to gain **wall-climbing superpowers**. For a class project, teen **Hibiki Kono** used inexpensive vacuums to create a climbing device that enables its wearer to **crawl up walls**. Just strap on the vacuums—which connect to two handheld suction pads that provide **super-sticking power** while the vacuum is running—and scale walls by releasing one pad at a time. Although Hibiki's mom put a height limit to his climbing, his teacher used the device to **hang** from the classroom ceiling!

PLANS ARE UNDER WAY FOR A SOLAR-POWERED PLANE THAT CAN FLY TO THE EDGE OF SPACE.

1

IN 1999, THE BREITLING ORBITER 3 HOT-AIR BALLOON FLEW NONSTOP AROUND THE WORLD.

2

SOLAR POWER HAS BEEN USED ON SPACECRAFT SINCE THE 1960S.

3

SOLAR**IMPULSE**

SOLAR CELLS

SUN-POWERED PLANE

Soar around the globe on the **power of sunshine** in a plane called the **Solar Impulse.** Solar panels line nearly every inch of the plane's wingspan, **absorbing energy** from the sun and **storing it** in batteries that power four **electric propellers.** The plane completed its first overnight flight in 2010, **flying nonstop** for more than **26 hours.** This proved that the plane could harness enough solar power during the day to keep it flying through the night. A **one-seater** aircraft, the Solar Impulse is built to be as **lightweight** as possible. Even the pilot has a weight limit: 187 pounds (85 kg).

SLEEPING JACKET

Who knew that a jacket could do more than just keep you warm? With an Excubo, you can fight the chill *and* stay supercomfy whenever you need to catch some z's. The jacket's collar turns up to become a sleeping mask, the cuffs become mittens for your hands, and the lapels do double time as pillows to cushion your slumber. No need to slump over to sleep: Just tighten the sides of the jacket and snooze comfortably upright wherever you are. Sounds like the perfect way to tune out your pesky little siblings on your next family road trip.

BUS OF THE FUTURE

A trip to a big city is always fun. But the drive to get there can be annoying. Solution: the Superbus. Currently in development, this alternative transportation can travel up to 155 miles an hour (249 km/h). The superfast, battery-powered luxury bus picks up passengers near their homes and drops them where they want to go. The plan is for the Superbus to drive in its own special lane on the highway to avoid traffic, merging onto shared roads as it nears its destination. Inside, you choose between wide, comfy chairs or sports-car-type seats. Individual video screens provide entertainment. And because there are eight doors on each side that move up and down, passengers can get in and out without tripping over anyone.

RUSSELL'S INVENTOR, PICTURED HERE WITH PRESIDENT OBAMA, ORIGINALLY FIXED UP MOTORCYCLES.

REAL GIRAFFES LEARN TO STAND JUST 30 MINUTES AFTER BIRTH.

A REAL GIRAFFE'S TONGUE IS NEARLY TWO FEET (0.6 M) LONG!

ELECTRIC GIRAFFE

Russell the electric giraffe just may be the tallest guest to ever visit the White House. This 17-foot (5-m)-tall, 1,700-pound (770-kg) robot wowed President Barack Obama with its ability to walk, talk, and even giggle when its tickled. Handmade with melded metal, Russell interacts with people with the help of webcams in its eyes and special touch-sensitive sensors on its nose and under its chin—and it even lights up with flashing LEDs. You can also hitch a ride on Russell, which runs on a 12-horsepower hybrid fuel-engine motor. And with silver glittery lava lamps for horns, it's no wonder Russell's a hit wherever it roams, from rock concerts to the White House.

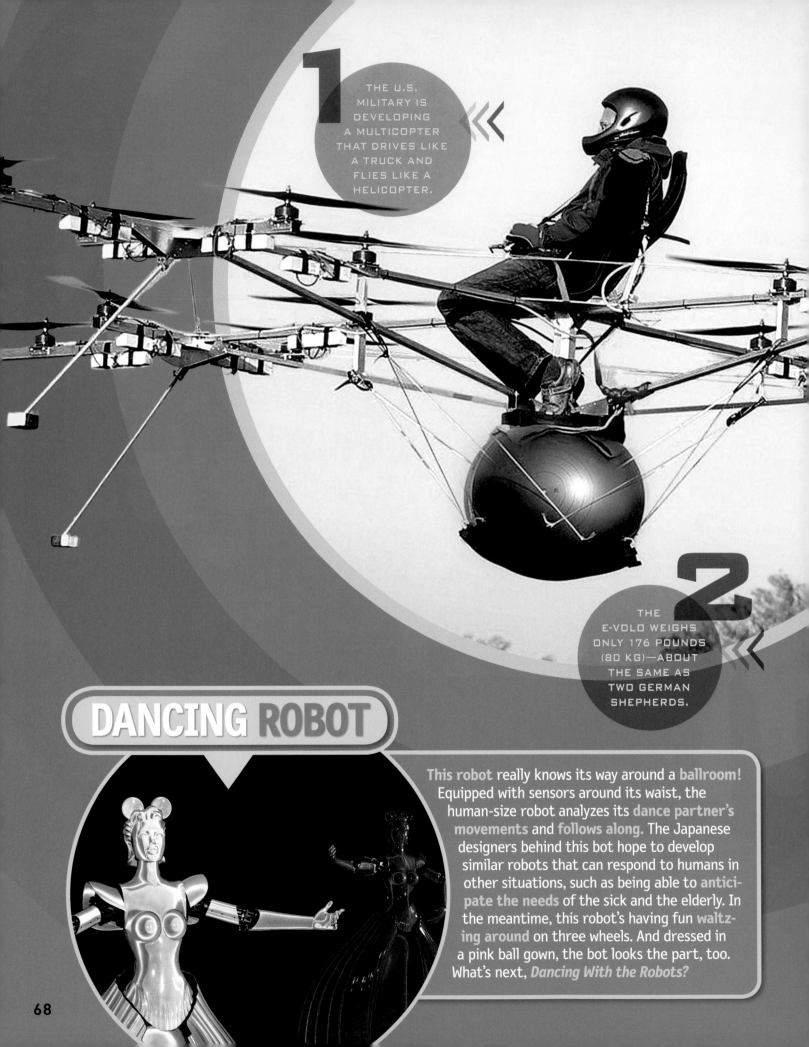

1 THE U.S. MILITARY IS DEVELOPING A MULTICOPTER THAT DRIVES LIKE A TRUCK AND FLIES LIKE A HELICOPTER.

2 THE E-VOLO WEIGHS ONLY 176 POUNDS (80 KG)—ABOUT THE SAME AS TWO GERMAN SHEPHERDS.

DANCING ROBOT

This robot really knows its way around a ballroom! Equipped with sensors around its waist, the human-size robot analyzes its dance partner's movements and follows along. The Japanese designers behind this bot hope to develop similar robots that can respond to humans in other situations, such as being able to anticipate the needs of the sick and the elderly. In the meantime, this robot's having fun waltzing around on three wheels. And dressed in a pink ball gown, the bot looks the part, too. What's next, *Dancing With the Robots?*

MULTICOPTER

What's got **16 rotors,** room for one, and runs on a battery pack? The **E-Volo electric multicopter!** This funky flying machine is said to be the world's first **"green"** helicopter in that it's emission free, using just electricity to take off, fly, and land. Designed by a German engineer, the **lightweight** copter operates with onboard computers that are controlled by a joystick. The current version of the E-Volo can fly for about **20 minutes,** but the goal is to get it in the air for up to an hour. And its creators claim that the E-Volo is **super-easy** to steer and control. So yes, maybe even a kid can pilot it ... one day.

FLOATING POOL

The rivers surrounding New York City may not be the most **ideal place to swim,** but a group of designers is hoping to change that. Their plan? To build a pool in the city's **East River** that will serve as a **giant filter** for the river water. Cleaning up to **500,000 gallons** (1.9 million L) a day, the pool's filters will remove **bacteria** and **harmful contaminants,** leaving nothing but fresh, clean, chemical-free H_2O to splash in. The **Olympic-size pool**—designed to fit nearly 500 people comfortably—will make for a lot of happy (and healthy) New Yorkers on a **hot summer day.**

RETRO PHONE

Talk about a throwback! The **iRetrophone** dials things way back by letting you dock your sleek and petite smartphone into a bulky **1950s-era telephone.** Aside from just looking cool, the iRetrophone lets you charge your battery while you chat into the receiver, **play music** from the built-in speakers, and walk and talk while using the wireless handset. So even though this phone seems old-fashioned, it still has a **modern ring to it.**

ROUND TREE HOUSES

Sleep among the **birds** in one of these amazing **eco-friendly tree houses.** Lofted in a towering tree about 120 feet (35 m) above Qualicum Beach on Vancouver Island in Canada, a **Free Spirit Sphere** is the perfect spot to be one with nature. You climb up a tree on a **spiral staircase** and cross a short suspension bridge to your sphere, which is secured in the branches with a thick web of rope. Once inside, enjoy **luxuries** such as electricity, running water, a refrigerator, and even built-in speakers to play your **favorite tunes.** Or, just lay back on the **double bed** and listen to the sounds of the birds and the **breeze.** Sure sounds like music to our ears!

1 THE BOAT'S TWO 9-GALLON (34-L) GASOLINE TANKS PROVIDE A 160-MILE (257-KM) RANGE.

2 THE FASTEST EVER SPEEDBOAT RECORDED A NECK-BREAKING 317 MILES AN HOUR (510 KM/H).

3 SEAPLANES—WHICH CAN TAKE OFF AND LAND ON WATER—ARE ALSO KNOWN AS FLYING BOATS.

FLYING BOAT

What do you get that **special someone** in your life who has *everything?* How about this **hovercraft!** Available for purchase for about **$200,000**, this **flying boat** can glide over land and water and soar up to 20 feet (6 m) in the air. Simply **push, pull, or twist** a joystick to accelerate, turn, and brake, while the hovercraft reaches speeds that can **surpass** a speeding car. Rough waters ahead? **No worries.** The craft can stay steady in winds of up to 25 miles an hour (40 km/h) and can tackle waves up to **6 feet (1.8 m) tall.** But it doesn't just operate on the seas: The hovercraft can skim over sand, swamps, and snow, too. Now that's what you call an **all-terrain vehicle!**

A 20-POUND (9-KG) DOG SHOULD DRINK AT LEAST 2 CUPS (473 ML) OF WATER DAILY.

SCIENTISTS HAVE PROVED THAT DOGS ARE SLOPPIER DRINKERS THAN CATS.

DOG WATER FOUNTAIN

Your dog can sit, fetch, and play dead, but can it **drink from a water fountain?** That trick is made simple for your pet with the **Pawcet**, which lets thirsty dogs get a drink whenever they want with the **touch of a paw**. Just hook the Pawcet up to your garden hose, and all your pup has to do is **step on the platform** to drink up cool, fresh water. Now that's something that'll really get your dog's tongue wagging.

TORPEDO TRICYLE

Imagine what your **friends would say** if you rode up to school in *this!* This **sleek** vehicle looks like a **mini race car**, but it's actually a specially adapted **recumbent** tricycle encased in a plastic shell. As you sit down and pedal away, the **aerodynamic shape** helps you go about **30 miles an hour** (49 km/h). Bonus: There's no need to hitch a ride on rainy days—the plastic **shell** also serves as a shelter from bad weather, keeping you warm and dry as you **zoom down the street.**

BIRD PHOTO BOOTH

Snap shots of **swallows** or capture **chickadees** as they eat with the Bird Photo Booth. Simply pop your phone or GoPro camera in the hidden enclosure in this **bird feeder**, then sneak into your house and **watch the birds chow down** in real time from a live feed on your computer or tablet. See the perfect shot? **Click away** as you get the ultimate up-close-and-personal pics of your **backyard birds**. But these aren't run-of-the-mill snaps: The Bird Photo Booth's high-quality **macro lens** enables your phone to take up close, **high-res** images that'll rival those of a real-life wildlife photographer. *Say Tweet!*

TENNIS COURTS WITH A SPLASH

What if you could hit a winning serve in **tennis** and then jump straight from the court **into the ocean to cool off**? It's not such a far-fetched idea if you play on a **floating tennis court**. The tennis players seen here were showing off their strokes in Mexico's **Acapulco Bay** before competing in a Mexican tournament. Sadly, a few tennis balls might get **lost in the water**, but you might argue that the ocean breezes are totally worth it.

VIDEO CHAT WITH YOUR DOG

Never stress over leaving your pup **home alone** again! Just turn on the **iCPooch** and you can **video chat** with little Chewy even if you're hundreds of miles away. Designed by a teen-ager who was seeking her own way to **check in on her pet** while at school, the iCPooch comes with a stand where you can plug your tablet into a **slobber-proof case.** When you want to check in, just open the iCPooch app on your phone and you'll be able to get **instant face time** with your **furry friend.** You can even reward your dog from afar by hitting a button in the app that'll automatically pop out a treat. **That's a good dog!**

SLIDE RIDER

Why walk down the stairs when you can *slide* down them? That's the idea behind the Slide Rider, a foldable mat that can be laid over a set of steps to create a giant slide from one floor of your house to another. The Slide Rider is made from the same sort of soft rubber you find in a gym class mat, and it can be unfolded whenever you feel like having a little fun. A bonus? The last mat is extra-cushioned to ensure a soft landing, which makes it *so* much more fun than sliding down the banister!

1 BUMPERS ENSURE THAT YOU DON'T SLIDE OUT AS YOU SLIDE DOWN.

2 THE SLIDE RIDER CAN ALSO BE USED OUTDOORS ON A HILL.

3 TRAVELERS PASSING THROUGH SINGAPORE'S CHANGI AIRPORT CAN SHOOT DOWN A FOUR-STORY TWISTY SLIDE!

THE WORLD'S LARGEST INFLATABLE STRUCTURE—A MODEL OF THE HUMAN BODY THAT PEOPLE CAN WALK INSIDE—IS NEARLY AS LONG AS A NEW YORK CITY BLOCK.

A DAREDEVIL ONCE WALKED ACROSS TWO CITY BLOCKS IN CHICAGO, U.S.A., ON A ¾-INCH- (1.9-CM)-THICK WIRE STRETCHED 588 FEET (179 M) IN THE AIR.

GIANT JUNGLE GYM

Move over, Spider-Man! There's no special sticky web required to **scale to the top** of this **crazy jungle gym**. All you need are your own hands and feet—and maybe a little courage, too. The contraption, called the **String Prototype**, is actually a giant **inflatable bubble** with endless amounts of sturdy string attached to the insides. As the bubble **fills with air**, it grows to **three stories tall** and the string inside stretches out and becomes sturdy enough to hold the weight of an adult. The best part? The whole thing can be deflated and packed away in **a matter of minutes**. So you may one day be able to, say, bring it over to your friend's house for your next playdate.

THE DESIGNERS ALSO CREATED ANOTHER INSTALLATION MADE OF LARGE CLIMBING NETS.

3

FACE PROTECTION
FROM SNOWSTORMS

1

In 1939, **somewhere** in Montreal, Canada, these **fashionable ladies** hit the streets showing off a short-lived idea for **keeping your face warm during snowstorms: a plastic cone!** You would strap it around your head to keep your face toasty and dry as the snow swirled around you. You could wear it with a **warm, fuzzy hat**—or simply by itself if you were worried about messing up your hair. It's hard to tell what happened to the cones, but one thing's for sure: This snow-stopping invention was a **bit of a flake.**

7 HAREBRAINED IDEAS FROM HISTORY

2

DONUT DUNKER

Times sure were different in the 1940s. This **wacky widget**, displayed at the **Congress of American Inventors** in Los Angeles, was designed so that commuters could **dunk their donuts** and **keep their hands free** to read the daily news. As an added bonus, this supersoaker also made sure that no **scalding hot** coffee touched your fingers as you dipped your donut. How *sweet!*

3

AMPHIBIOUS BIKE

This "**bubble bike**" really made waves when it debuted in Paris in 1932. The **amphibious** contraption was at home on both land and water. Called the **Cyclomer**, the bike's two large, drum-shaped and **hollow wheels** doubled as **floats** for water cycling. The smaller, movable floats (shown here in the "land" position) could be lowered to water level to give the bike extra stability. This rider wouldn't have even needed to change out of his suit and tie and into a swimsuit before he **hit the lake**.

4 CAR SAFETY

Even before cars had so many technological safety features, early automotive designers had an eye out for safety. This car came equipped with a mesh platform attached to the front to scoop up careless pedestrians. The design was meant to reduce the number of people killed in car accidents.

5
ALL-TERRAIN VEHICLE

Ever since the **early days** of the car, people have been itching to go where roads **weren't meant to take them.** This giant **off-road** vehicle could travel down slopes up to **65 degrees.** It looks like this bulky beast paved the way for today's rugged ATVs.

EARLY GPS

6

Today, **global positioning systems (GPSs)** help drivers know where to go without having to get out a **paper map**. This early version of a GPS used a much more **low-tech** method—a rolling map. The machine connected to a car's dashboard and displayed a map that **rolled at the same rate** as the car.

RADIO HAT

This guy would have **loved** the iPod! It wasn't long after the invention of radio broadcasts that people tried to take their **clunky radios** with them. This portable radio was built into a straw hat, picking up **radio signals** right above your head. It came complete with a **horn** to deliver the sounds to you.

7

COOL CONVERTIBLE

It's a car with **built-in sunglasses!** The Ferrari **Superamerica** convertible features a transparent roof—like a window. But what if you've had enough sun? Just use the **automatic dimmer** to change the glass roof from clear to dark in under a minute. The car also **sets the speed record** for the world's fastest-opening top. It takes just ten seconds for the roof to lift up and flip back. The Ferrari can reach nearly **200 miles an hour** (322 km/h), making it the speediest convertible ever—a perfect spy getaway car!

THE ROBOT'S KICK IS SO POWERFUL, IT CAN REDUCE A CINDER BLOCK TO DUST.

2

ALL-SEASONS SLED

No snow? No problem! Just hop on the **Slicer** and you can sled no matter the weather. Simply **fill** the sled's two trays **with water** and **pop them into the freezer.** Once they're frozen solid, snap the ice blocks into place on the bottom of the sled and head for the hills. Depending on how hot it is outside, the **ice blocks** will stay solid for about **two hours** before melting. Oh, and you can use the Slicer in the winter, too—just remove the trays. **Cool!**

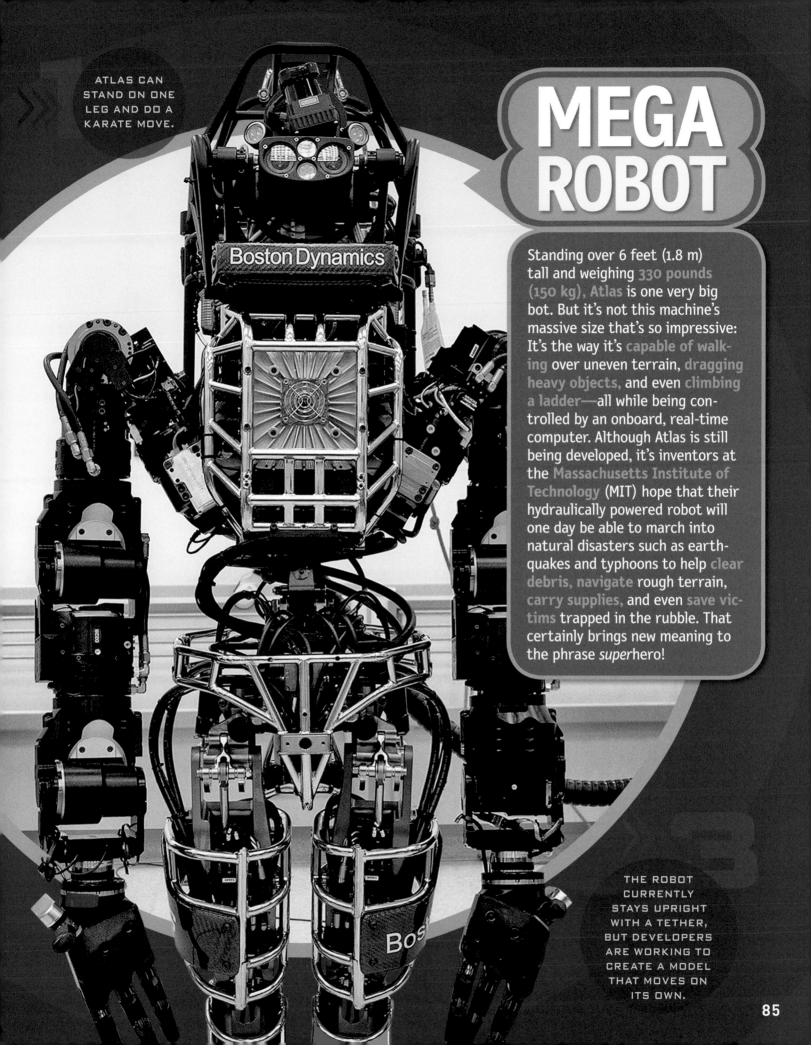

ATLAS CAN STAND ON ONE LEG AND DO A KARATE MOVE.

MEGA ROBOT

Standing over 6 feet (1.8 m) tall and weighing **330 pounds (150 kg), Atlas** is one very big bot. But it's not this machine's massive size that's so impressive: It's the way it's **capable of walking** over uneven terrain, **dragging heavy objects,** and even **climbing a ladder**—all while being controlled by an onboard, real-time computer. Although Atlas is still being developed, it's inventors at the **Massachusetts Institute of Technology** (MIT) hope that their hydraulically powered robot will one day be able to march into natural disasters such as earthquakes and typhoons to help **clear debris, navigate** rough terrain, **carry supplies,** and even **save victims** trapped in the rubble. That certainly brings new meaning to the phrase *super*hero!

THE ROBOT CURRENTLY STAYS UPRIGHT WITH A TETHER, BUT DEVELOPERS ARE WORKING TO CREATE A MODEL THAT MOVES ON ITS OWN.

1 THE HOVERBIKE HAS A SIMILAR DESIGN TO THE SPEEDER BIKE FROM THE ORIGINAL STAR WARS MOVIES.

2 IT'S CAPABLE OF FOLDING TO A THIRD OF ITS SIZE.

3 THE HOVERBIKE CAN BE FLOWN WITH OR WITHOUT A PILOT.

BIKE TAKES FLIGHT

The Hoverbike has a seat and handlebars just like a motorcycle, but this contraption travels to a place you could never reach on a regular hog—**the sky!** Just twist the throttle and take off! Two **large propellers** on the bike's front and back launch it off the ground. Turn the handlebars to steer the craft **through the air.** And don't worry if you run into trouble on the skyway—**parachutes** mounted to the bike pop open in an emergency, allowing you to float safely back to earth. Although still being tested, Australian inventor Chris Malloy claims that the Hoverbike will be able to reach speeds of **173 miles an hour** (278 km/h) and **climb to 10,000 feet** (3,048 m). Talk about getting a lift!

SMART PJs

These PJs **aren't just cozy**—they're **clever, too!** Each of the pajamas's **unique dot patterns** triggers a story or fable when you **scan it** with a smartphone. Just **wave your phone** over the dots and connect to a free app that'll deliver a quick brothers Grimm **bedtime story** or a classic fairy tale such as *Cinderella.* Would you rather read the story yourself? Mute the narrator and read from your smartphone instead. There are also featured animals, so scanning some sets of dots will reveal pictures of different species and **fun facts,** too. The coolest part? The app's content **changes regularly,** so it's like a new pair of PJs with every update. Let's just hope you don't grow out of them too fast!

LIGHT-UP PILLOW

Getting startled out of a deep sleep by the **shrill sounds** of an alarm clock is probably your **least favorite** part of the day. But with the **Glo Pillow** you can silence those rude awakenings for good. Thanks to a built-in **grid of LED lights,** the Glo Pillow **mimics a natural sunrise** by gradually brightening your bedroom. Set the alarm before bed, and the pillow will emit a gentle light starting **40 minutes** before your scheduled wake-up time. Experts say the process helps you **naturally** ease out of sleep, guaranteeing a truly good morning.

TREE TENT

If a **giant spider** spun a camping tent, it would look like a **Tentsile**. This **portable shelter** lets you get up and away from it all. Made of **sturdy** nylon, it's designed to hang between trees rather than rest on the cold, lumpy ground. Inside, campers sleep in **comfy hammocks** without rocks or roots digging into their backs. Tentsiles come in several sizes, including a three-person model that you can connect to other Tentsiles. You can even replace the tent's floor with a **trampoline** to create the ultimate playground. Way to be a **happy camper**!

"TELEPORTATION" POD

You and your buddy *really* want to play today. Only problem? He's visiting relatives **six states away**. With the **TeleHuman** video conferencing pod, you can still hang with him in your house ... kind of. Using six **special sensors**, a **3-D projector**, and a **mirror**, this six-foot (1.8-m)-tall cylindrical pod creates a life-size **hologram** of anyone you choose to video chat with. And with a **360-degree view**, you can walk around to see your friend from all angles. It's *almost* as cool as him **actually teleporting** to you. Almost.

THE BIKE HAS RECHARGEABLE HEAD AND TAIL LIGHTS.

THE BIKE'S NICKNAME IS COBI.

7-SEATER BIKE

Forget carpooling: Next time you and your buddies are heading to school together, just **hop on a ConferenceBike** instead! This **social cycle** sits seven in a **circle**, with everyone facing each other. **One person steers,** while everyone pedals together to get to your destination. Hitching a ride on the **400-pound** (180-kg) conference bike may not be as quick as your car—top speed is around **10 miles an hour** (16 km/h)—but you'll be cutting down on icky emissions that harm the environment. Score!

GOOGLE USES THESE BIKES AT THEIR HEADQUARTERS IN MOUNTAIN VIEW, CALIFORNIA, U.S.A.

1

THE FUTURE STRAWSCRAPER IS CURRENTLY ONE OF SWEDEN'S TALLEST APARTMENT BUILDINGS.

2

THERE ARE PLANS TO INCLUDE A RESTAURANT AND A VIEWING PLATFORM IN THE STRAWSCRAPER.

3

AN ITALIAN ARTIST CREATES 3-D SCULPTURES USING TENS OF THOUSANDS OF DRINKING STRAWS!

THE STRAWSCRAPER

For some people, a windy day is a bad hair day. But for the folks designing this odd-looking building, a windy day is a good hair day. For them, **windy days** will mean the **hairy fibers** on their building are capturing loads of **free energy!** A Swedish architectural firm is working on plans to transform an existing Stockholm building into a futuristic **40-floor** skyscraper that will create energy. The design for this project, known as the **Strawscraper,** encloses the building in a casing covered with long, **flexible straws** that turn **wind motion** into **electrical energy.** From gentle breezes to strong winds, the friction on the straws will produce and store electricity much like a wind power plant does. The Strawscraper will be much **quieter** than a wind turbine, though, and it will be **bird friendly,** too. (Birds sometimes fly into the blades of wind turbines.) Although still in the planning stages, it's clear that the Strawscraper—shown here in concept form—will stand out. As the fringe whips in the wind, this "hairway" to heaven will seem to be a living, breathing thing!

DESKTOP 3-D SCANNER

1 DIGITIZE

2 PRINT

So, you and your little brother are fighting over that toy … *again?* Just pull out the **MakerBot Digitizer** and you can have a **digital copy** of your object in minutes. This desktop gadget can scan **almost anything,** as long as it's **less than eight inches** (20 cm) in diameter. Just place your item on the **rotating turntable,** and the Digitizer uses lasers and a webcam to create a **3-D digital file** in less than 15 minutes. Then take the file, shoot it over to a **3-D printer,** and replicate that toy quicker than you can say, "But he's not sharing!"

BENDY BIKE

Here's one way to confuse a bike thief: Wrap your bike around a pole! Bendy bikes let you do just that, thanks to a frame that's flexible enough to wrap around lampposts and **street signs.** A design student, hoping to decrease the staggering number of bikes stolen each year, came up with this **clever cycle** that looks like a regular bike when you're riding it. Once you're ready to lock it up, however, you loosen a cable below the seat and the bike **splits** into two segments so you can bend the frame up to **180 degrees.** Next, you can secure it to a pole with a regular bike lock, leaving would-be thieves **scratching their heads.**

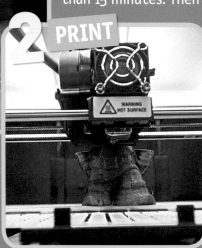

CAR WITH SPIN

Talk about **going for a spin**: The **Nissan Pivo** is a futuristic car that can **rotate 360 degrees** to face any direction. Let's say that you're on a trip and see something amazing: surfers getting extreme on a giant wave or a bear alongside the road. **Instead of craning your neck** to look at what's going on, you stop the car, press a button, and **rotate** the Pivo so that everyone gets a **perfect view** of the action. How convenient! The Pivo also sports other **high-tech tricks**. If your favorite song is on the radio, you can turn it up just by motioning upward with your hands!

1 NO GAS REQUIRED! THE PIVO IS AN ALL-ELECTRIC CAR.

2 A ROBOTIC AGENT CHATS WITH YOU THROUGH THE CAR'S CONSOLE.

3 THE PIVO OFFERS ROOM FOR THREE PASSENGERS.

1
THE SUIT WAS ORIGINALLY DESIGNED TO HELP SOLDIERS GAIN AN EDGE ON THE BATTLEFIELD.

THE COMPANY IS ALSO DEVELOPING AN EXOSKELETON FOR INJURED CHILDREN.
2

WALKING EXOSKELETON

3
SOME SPECIES SUCH AS GRASSHOPPERS AND LOBSTERS HAVE EXOSKELETONS, WHICH SUPPORT AND PROTECT THEIR BODIES.

When a skiing accident left Amanda Boxtel paralyzed from the waist down, she didn't think she'd ever walk again. But with the help of an Ekso bionic suit, Boxtel is back on her feet. Considered a "wearable robot," this exoskeleton has sensors that pick up upper-body movements in its users, which activate battery-powered motors in the robotic legs. So, slowly but surely, people like Boxtel can learn to take solo strides by leaning forward or to one side. While the Ekso suit isn't a way to cure paralysis for good, it's certainly a step in the right direction.

SELF-DRIVING TOY CAR

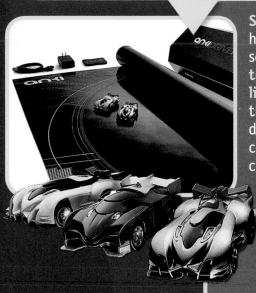

Self-driving cars may not be on the roads yet, but here's a start: toy race cars that, well, race by themselves! The Anki DRIVE racing game uses **robotic toy cars** equipped with **microprocessors, infrared lights, and cameras** to cruise around the track on their own. Line up the cars on a **special mat** (embedded with positioning info so the cars never veer off course) and watch them race each other. Up for a challenge? Race a robot by using your **smartphone or tablet** to control a car. With special sensors that feed data to your smart gadget, your car can **swerve** in and out of lanes, make **wide or narrow turns,** and even **smash** into a competitor. That robot never saw you coming!

AIR UMBRELLA

Here's a way to *really* make the rain, rain go away: **Blast it right off of you!** Instead of simply shielding you from the weather like your basic umbrella, this gadget doesn't even let the raindrops come close. A powerful **blast of air** shoots through the umbrella and up above you, creating a force field that acts like an **invisible canopy** to keep you **totally dry.** The battery-operated umbrella is standard size and will easily slip into your backpack. So you can, you know, save it for a rainy day.

THE SEATCASE

It's a suitcase, it's a seat ... **it's a Seatcase!** Next time you're passing through an airport and need to rest your feet, just **pop out the seat** attached to your rolling suitcase and **sit down.** Any suitcase can turn into a convenient chair; just hook this special, **lightweight steel attachment** to your bag and flip out a canvas seat whenever you want. The Seatcase was developed by a former politician in the United Kingdom after he spent **many hours** waiting—and standing—at train stations and airports. If only it could *pack* your suitcase for you, too!

BUBBLE TENT

Sleep **outside** without being bitten by bugs or waking up with a backache. **CristalBubble** tents are clear, inflatable shelters that have beds, floors, and electricity. The tents come in many sizes, and continuous airflow generated by turbines **keeps them inflated,** so you can have as many friends along as you want. For more privacy, a few models are **see-through** only on the top. This kind of camping is not exactly roughing it—but what a great way to watch for nocturnal critters or to check out a **meteor shower.**

MECHANICAL PIG

Pigs may **never be able to fly,** but try telling that to Adrian Wareham. The British farmer and engineer created **Pigasus,** a mechanical oinker that—yep—can take flight. Kind of. The winged wonder, powered by a motorbike's engine and made of **scrap metal,** is able to clear about seven inches (18 cm) of air as it bounces along the road. But Wareham doesn't just do pigs: He also created a ride-along dog and a cow that can walk on all fours at speeds of about **ten miles an hour** (16 km/h). Now that's *moo*-ving.

1 THE AIRPOD CAN REACH SPEEDS OF UP TO 43 MILES AN HOUR (69 KM/H).

2 ONE TANK OF AIR LASTS LONGER THAN 125 MILES (200 KM) AND TAKES ONLY TWO MINUTES TO FILL UP.

3 PLANS ARE UNDER WAY FOR A TRUCK, CONVERTIBLE, AND BUS VERSION OF THE AIRPOD.

RUNNING ON AIR

Tell Dad to **leave the minivan at home**—you'll look so much cooler when you pull up to school in one of these. The appropriately named **AIRPod** runs on **compressed air**. Unlike gasoline-powered cars, it produces **zero pollution** and actually emits air that's cleaner than the stuff you breathe every day. Designed for scooting around town, the **itty-bitty** AIRPod has four wheels and three seats (one in front, two in back). Like a regular car, it has an accelerator and a brake pedal on the floor. But instead of a steering wheel, the AIRPod has a **joystick**. If you know how to **play a video game**, you know how to **make this little car turn**. Simply push the stick left or right. There is no reverse, so spin the car around by holding the joystick all the way to the right or to the left. Let's see your parents' minivan do *that*.

SCOOTER STROLLER

On-the-go moms and dads can really pick up the pace with this **speedy stroller**, which works double duty as **a scooter**. Running late for a play-date? Pull a lever at the bottom of the stroller and a scooter **platform pops out**. Hop on and steer the stroller by leaning left or right. With enough momentum (and a little downhill, too), the stroller can go pretty fast. **Don't worry**—the stroller comes equipped with **hydraulic hand brakes**, so the little one stays safe and sound.

BIONIC CONTACT LENS

Researchers are developing **contact lenses** that may one day help **blind people see**. Outfitted with electrodes, the lenses—worn like regular contacts—get signals **from a camera**, either on a smartphone or attached to one's glasses. When a user looks or points the camera at an object such as a door or a dog, the camera **translates the digital image** into small electronic impulses felt on the outer part of the eye. According to researchers, these sensations produce a result **similar to reading braille**, but with the eyes instead of the fingertips.

ULTRACOMPACT VEHICLE

Thrilled with the ride, you zip along on the **smallest, coolest looking** vehicle ever. Instead of front and back wheels, its two wheels are **side by side**—and just **inches apart.** From the side, it looks like a unicycle from the future. It's the **Uno,** a vehicle much smaller and more maneuverable than even a motorcycle. The Uno is **electric,** so it doesn't pollute, and its top speed is about **15 miles an hour** (24 km/h). An internal, high-tech **gyroscope,** controlled by body movements, keeps you balanced. **Lean forward** to accelerate, to the side to turn, and backward to stop. The Uno's inventor? **An 18-year-old** inspired to build a nonpolluting way to get around.

THE HAILFIRE DROID IN STAR WARS IS A DICYCLE.

THE UNO IS A TYPE OF DICYCLE—A VEHICLE WITH TWO SIDE-BY-SIDE WHEELS.

THE COMPANY HAS ALSO INVENTED A COMBO OF A SKATEBOARD, MOTOCROSS BIKE, AND TANK.

3

FUTURE WHEELS

Bikes and skateboards are so yesterday! Toyota's electric-powered i-unit is a personal transporter designed to create a new, comfy way to get around. In low-speed mode, you drive the i-unit in an upright position. In high-speed mode, it reclines for better handling. The driver uses a simple hand controller. Push to go forward, twist to turn right or left, and pull or let go to stop. Designed to be environmentally friendly, the lightweight i-unit is made partly of material from plants!

1 THE DESIGN AND CONCEPT WERE INSPIRED BY A TREE LEAF.

2 YOU CAN CUSTOMIZE YOUR I-UNIT TO FLASH YOUR FAVORITE COLORS AS YOU DRIVE.

3 THE I-UNIT WEIGHS ABOUT AS MUCH AS AN ADULT AFRICAN LION.

ESCAPE POD

There's nothing wrong with wanting a little **personal space.** And that's exactly what the **Escape Pod** delivers. At first glance, this wacky seat looks like a giant felt flower, but once you pull up the chair's "petals," you create your own cocoon. Plus, the pod's center consists of a giant beanbag, meaning you'll be completely comfy as you slip into that secret spot that's all your own.

NAP CABIN

An airport **may not be** the coziest place to take a catnap. Unless, that is, you're in a **Napcab sleeping cabin**—a personal snoozing spot located in Germany's Munich Airport. For about **$12 an hour,** weary travelers can rent a 43-square-foot (4-sq-m) cabin and tuck into a bed until it's time to catch a flight. And if you're worried about missing your boarding time? Just **set an alarm** for whenever you want to wake up. Internet access, air-conditioning, and a **touch-screen TV** loaded with movies and shows make the cabin even cozier. Bet you wish there was a Napcab in your school, too!

FISH (TOILET) TANK

The next time you go to the bathroom, **don't forget the fish food.** The Fish 'n Flush turns a regular toilet into an **aquarium.** Two see-through tanks attach to the toilet. The **inner tank** is what flushes the toilet. Surrounding that tank is an aquarium. When you flush, the water level of the inner tank goes down, making it seem as if water is emptying from your aquarium. Don't worry—**it's an illusion.** The fish tank's water level remains the same, so **your fishies are fine.**

DANCING EGG

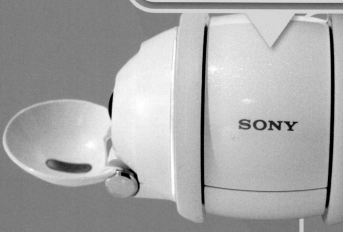

This is an **MP3 player** that loves to rock and roll. Press the play button and the **Rolly** comes alive—blasting songs and spinning and **dancing to the beat,** as well as flashing a rainbow of **lights.** It's got a pretty sweet set of moves, from wheels that allow it to **roll around** a desk or floor to "shoulders" and "arms" that jig in time to the music. The Rolly knows how to shake it on its own, or you can **choreograph routines** to different songs, orchestrating everything from how the **lights flash** to the way it moves its limbs. It's like having a **dance partner** as you bop around the room to your favorite tunes!

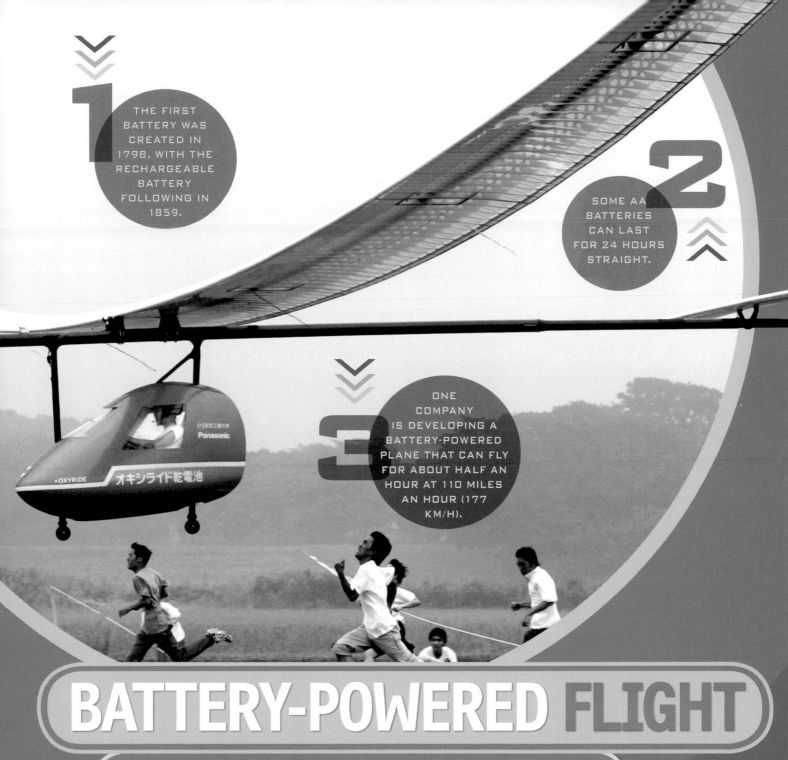

1
THE FIRST BATTERY WAS CREATED IN 1798, WITH THE RECHARGEABLE BATTERY FOLLOWING IN 1859.

2
SOME AA BATTERIES CAN LAST FOR 24 HOURS STRAIGHT.

3
ONE COMPANY IS DEVELOPING A BATTERY-POWERED PLANE THAT CAN FLY FOR ABOUT HALF AN HOUR AT 110 MILES AN HOUR (177 KM/H).

BATTERY-POWERED FLIGHT

You've probably heard of battery-powered cars—popular because they **reduce** dependence on expensive, **pollution-producing fuel**. But what about an airplane powered by batteries? The **Oxyflyer** is the first plane to take to the sky on traditional batteries alone. Using 160 special **high-powered AA batteries**, the Oxyflyer stayed in the air for 59 seconds and covered 1,284 feet (391 m), or about a **quarter of a mile** (beating the Wright brothers' record of 852 feet [260 m] in 1903). Because batteries tend to add a lot of weight, the Oxyflyer is designed to be lightweight, with a sprawling **100-foot (30.5-m) wingspan** to give it more lift. Now that the Oxyflyer has proven it's possible to fly this way, the **efficient aircraft** has inspired other environmentally friendly planes. So someday you'll be able to fly *green* skies!

TOPSY-TURVY RIDE

You'll literally roll on the ground laughing with the **Buzzball.** Take a seat, strap yourself in, and press the two **hand triggers to get rolling.** Each trigger is connected to a separate motor that powers two wheels under the chair. You and the seat remain **mostly upright,** but as the wheels start to spin, the Buzzball begins to roll. **To steer,** press one of the triggers. That prompts the wheel on one side to turn, causing the Buzzball to roll in **that direction.** Depending on how fast you're going, the ball simply turns, or it **tumbles** around multiple times. It's like being on a **roller coaster,** motion simulator, and skateboard half-pipe all at once.

BED ROCKS

Forget kicking back on the couch. The best seat in your house might be a **pile of rocks**—as long as those rocks are **Livingstones.** These **plush pillows** look just like small boulders. They come in a variety of colors and sizes, from small decorative pebble cushions to **stone-shaped sofas.** Pile them into a mini-mountain to bring an outdoorsy feel to your living room, and then surprise your pals by plopping down **without bruising your behind.** Arrange the cushions into a bed, and you just might "rock" yourself to sleep.

FLYBOARD

Get some **major air** with the help of a **Flyboard,** a water jet pack. This cool contraption connects to a Jet Ski and uses powerful **streams of water** to shoot you as high as a **three-story building.** How does it work? First, you strap the Flyboard to your feet and get in the water. Have a friend **rev up** the Jet Ski as the hose sucks in about **5,000 gallons (18,927 L) of water per minute.** The Flyboard then shoots the water beneath you. The resulting column of water launches you way above the waves. Fearless Flyboarders can do **dolphin dives,** double backflips, **spins,** and **barrel rolls.** But it's cool if you just want to coast along and enjoy the view from the top.

INDEX

INDEX

CREDITS

CREDITS

Staff for This book
Ariane Szu-Tu, *Project Manager*
Sarah Wassner Flynn, *Project Editor*
Julide Dengel, *Art Director*
Lisa Jewell, *Photo Editor*
Simon Renwick, *Designer*
Paige Towler, *Editorial Assistant*
Sanjida Rashid, *Design Production Assistant*
Michael Cassady, *Rights Clearance Specialist*
Erica Holsclaw, *Special Projects Assistant*
Rachel Kenny, *Special Projects Assistant*
Grace Hill, *Managing Editor*
Mike O'Connor, *Production Editor*
Lewis R. Bassford, *Production Manager*
Darrick McRae, *Manager, Production Services*
Susan Borke, *Legal and Business Affairs*
Neal Edwards, *Imaging*

Contributing Writers: Crispin Boyer, Laura Daily, Michelle Harris, Cathy Lu, Sean McCollum, Douglas E. Richards, Sarah Wassner Flynn

Based on the "Cool Inventions" Department in *National Geographic Kids* **Magazine**
Rachel Buchholz, *Editor and Vice President*
Andrea Silen, *Associate Editor*
Lisa Jewell, *Photo Editor*
Julide Dengel, *Designer*
Stephanie Rudig, *Associate Digital Designer*
Rose Davidson, *Special Projects Assistant*
Nick Spagnoli, *Copy Editor*

Published by the National Geographic Society
Gary E. Knell, *President and CEO*
John M. Fahey, *Chairman of the Board*
Melina Gerosa Bellows, *Chief Education Officer*
Declan Moore, *Chief Media Officer*
Hector Sierra, *Senior Vice President and General Manager, Book Division*

Senior Management Team, Kids Publishing and Media Nancy Laties Feresten, *Senior Vice President*; Jennifer Emmett, *Vice President, Editorial Director, Kids Books*; Julie Vosburgh Agnone, *Vice President, Editorial Operations*; Rachel Buchholz, *Editor and Vice President, NG Kids magazine*; Michelle Sullivan, *Vice President, Kids Digital*; Eva Absher-Schantz, *Design Director*; Jay Sumner, *Photo Director*; Hannah August, *Marketing Director*; R. Gary Colbert, *Production Director*

Digital Anne McCormack, *Director*; Laura Goertzel, Sara Zeglin, *Producers*; Jed Winer, *Special Projects Assistant*; Emma Rigney, *Creative Producer*; Brian Ford, *Video Producer*; Bianca Bowman, *Assistant Producer*; Natalie Jones, *Senior Product Manager*

The National Geographic Society is one of the world's largest nonprofit scientific and educational organizations. Founded in 1888 to "increase and diffuse geographic knowledge," the Society's mission is to inspire people to care about the planet. It reaches more than 400 million people worldwide each month through its official journal, *National Geographic*, and other magazines; National Geographic Channel; television documentaries; music; radio; films; books; DVDs; maps; exhibitions; live events; school publishing programs; interactive media; and merchandise. National Geographic has funded more than 10,000 scientific research, conservation, and exploration projects and supports an education program promoting geographic literacy.

For more information, please visit nationalgeographic.com, call 1-800-NGS LINE (647-5463), or write to the following address:
National Geographic Society
1145 17th Street N.W.
Washington, D.C. 20036-4688 U.S.A.

Visit us online at nationalgeographic.com/books

For librarians and teachers: ngchildrensbooks.org

More for kids from National Geographic: kids.nationalgeographic.com

For information about special discounts for bulk purchases, please contact National Geographic Books Special Sales: ngspecsales@ngs.org

For rights or permissions inquiries, please contact National Geographic Books Subsidiary Rights: ngbookrights@ngs.org

Paperback ISBN: 978-1-4263-1885-6
Reinforced library binding ISBN: 978-1-4263-1886-3

Printed in the United States of America
15/CK-CML/1